lonely planet

POCKET
HAMBURG

Barbara Woolsey

Contents

Above: Hamburg skyline including St Michaelis Kirche (p58)
Below: Elbmeile (p130)

Plan Your Trip   4

The Journey Begins Here 4
Our Picks 6
Perfect Days 18
Get Prepared 22
When To Go 24
Getting There 26
Getting Around 27
A Few Surprises 30

POCKET **HAMBURG**

Explore Hamburg   33

Altstadt	35
Neustadt	55
St Georg	71
Speicherstadt & HafenCity	85
St Pauli & the Reeperbahn	103
Altona & the Elbmeile	127

Hamburg Toolkit   143

Family Travel	144
Accommodation	145
Food, Drink & Nightlife	146
LGBTIQ+ Travellers	148
Health & Safe Travel	149
Responsible Travel	150
Accessible Travel	152
Nuts & Bolts	153
Language	154
Index	156

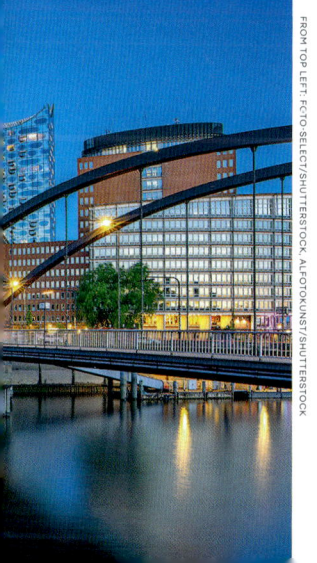

FROM TOP LEFT: FOTO-SELECT/SHUTTERSTOCK, ALFOTOKUNST/SHUTTERSTOCK

★ Top Experiences

Rathaus	38
Mahnmal St Nikolai	40
Hamburger Kunsthalle	43
St Michaelis Kirche	58
Alsterarkaden	61
KomponistenQuartier	62
Museum für Kunst und Gewerbe	74
Internationales Maritimes Museum	87
Miniatur Wunderland	88
Elbphilharmonie	89
Fischmarkt	106
Hamburg Bunker	109
Elbmeile	130

The Journey Begins Here

I'm fascinated by Hamburg's extremes. Germany's second-largest city changes from gritty to glam in only blocks; the best parts encompass the grand, neo-Renaissance Rathaus and the striking, glass-clad Elbphilharmonie glinting off the Elbe River. And then on the other hand, the Reeperbahn with its clubs and dive bars is an assault on all senses by night – and after sunrise. Excesses say much about Hamburg's tendency to be fearless, rebellious and future-orientated. Both rough and refined, it has a little something for every type of traveller.

Barbara Woolsey
@xo.babxi
Barbara is a Canadian travel writer who has lived in Germany since 2013. When she's not working for Lonely Planet she can be found DJing in Berlin's best clubs.

Rathaus (p38)
FOTO-SELECT/SHUTTERSTOCK

THE BEST

Panoramic Experiences

Hamburg's architectural excellence has its roots in devastation and rejuvenation: WWII's destruction of the city's centre and the contemporary transformation of the harbour. From the tips of church spires to high-rise rooftops, breathtaking panoramas are everywhere.

Ascend the sole surviving remnant of the bomb-razed **Mahnmal St Nikolai**, its sky-high, neo-Gothic spire. Afterwards, descend into its war-memorial crypt museum. (p40)

Zip in the lift up to the viewing platform of Hamburg's largest church, **St Michaelis Kirche** (pictured above left). The harbour vistas from here just can't be beat. (p58)

Take the tucked-away stairwell to the rooftop terrace at **Dockland** for a serene perspective on bustling harbour life. It's Hamburg's most hidden panoramic experience. (p131)

Endure the 300-some steps to the monolithic **Hamburg Bunker** (pictured above right) for landmark views: Hamburg's tallest building, St Pauli's beloved football stadium and more. (p109)

Gaze out from the dizzying, 360-degree observation deck at the **Elbphilharmonie**. This is truly Hamburg's quintessential panoramic experience – and it's free. (p89)

Right: Elbphilharmonie (p89; architects Herzog and de Meuron), HafenCity

FROM LEFT: SAIKO3P/SHUTTERSTOCK, SON-MEDIA/SHUTTERSTOCK, FOTO-SELECT/SHUTTERSTOCK

PLAN YOUR TRIP

THE BEST
Food Experiences

Virtually every part of Hamburg has good dining, and the options range from humble to haute. Unsurprisingly, seafood is the port city's speciality: *Fischbrötchen* (fish sandwiches) prove that even simple, affordable dishes can be truly satisfying.

Let a beer sommelier take you on a 'brewed awakening' – craft beer pairings tailored to your preference and meal – at **Altes Mädchen**. (p138)

Indulge in the best *Labskaus* (meat, fish, beetroot and potato stew; pictured above) at the 1795-established **Old Commercial Room**. Even if Hamburg's most beloved dish isn't your thing, the ambience is delectable. (p68)

Lap up rustic regional dishes such as *Pannfisch* (fried fish) and *Frikadelle* (meat patties) at tilting former dockworkers' canteen **Oberhafen Kantine**. (p96)

Nibble fish sandwiches of every kind at the **Fischmarkt**: *Nordseekrabben* (brown shrimp), *Matjes* (young herring; pictured above) or the most beloved *Backfisch* (battered and fried white fillet; p106).

Touch, smell and taste rare herbs and seasonings at **Spicy's Gewürzmuseum**. The olfactory extravaganza harks back to Hamburg's trading days. (p97)

Mojo Club (p119), St Pauli

THE BEST

Musical Experiences

Hamburg's vibrant entertainment scene is among the most diverse you'll find anywhere. From famous classical music venues to the down and dirty stages of St Pauli, there's always a performance to enjoy.

Vibe to live instrumentals while sipping whisky – Hamburg's underground jazz den **Mojo Club** always hits the right notes. (p119)

Attend a concert at the world-famous **Elbphilharmonie** for a rich experience that takes in a sleek architectural setting and state-of-the-art acoustics. (p89)

Play through classical music history at the **KomponistenQuartier**, where historic homes turned museums celebrate Brahms and Mendelssohn, and peer into luthiers' studios. (p62)

Let loose at alt-rock from indie to punk at the renowned **Molotow**. Bands from the White Stripes to the Black Keys have gone big after gigging here. (p120)

Indulge in a grand evening of Verdi or Strauss at the **Staatsoper**. Tickets to Hamburg's world-renowned opera house can often be found for a comparatively low price. (p66)

THE BEST
Gallery Experiences

Major art galleries and smaller private spaces intermingle in Hamburg to create a dynamic scene. The city's Kunstmeile (Art Mile) offers sightseeing across five contemporary galleries in an excellent-value combo ticket.

Feast your eyes on the **Hamburger Kunsthalle**, a world-class affair spanning Renaissance to modern and the work of greats from Monet to Warhol. (p43)

Gaze at 600,000 handicrafts, some dating back thousands of years, at the **Museum für Kunst und Gewerbe** (pictured above right) – the collection includes furniture, porcelain, Japanese posters and pop art. (p74)

Wander the echoey brick interiors of **Deichtorhallen** (pictured above left), showcasing high-profile modern art. A hip shipping container displays photography while part of the museum is being renovated. (p47)

Have a surprisingly contemporary experience at Hamburg's oldest art space, the **Galerie Commeter**. Painting, graphics and sculpture abound. (p48)

Creep around **Harry's Hamburger Hafenbasar & Museum** on a docked vessel to see (sometimes very) unusual cultural artefacts with an artistic side. (p95)

Right: Hamburger Kunsthalle (p43), Altstadt
FROM LEFT: FOTO-SELECT/SHUTTERSTOCK, PHILLIP KRASKOFF SHUTTERSTOCK, DATENSCHUTZ-STOCKFOTO/SHUTTERSTOCK

THE BEST
Market Experiences

Hamburg counts a couple of big, chaotic markets among its most popular attractions. Meanwhile, smaller neighbourhood markets offer a different kind of exploration: leisurely vibes and an authentic reflection of local life.

Sit back in a container beer garden at St Pauli's Wednesday **Nachtmarkt** (night market). Fragrant food, draft craft brews and live bands are an intoxicating mix. (p117)

Pack a picnic basket of artisan treats at St Georg's Friday **Wochenmarkt**. Some of Hamburg's best people watching is a plus. (p78)

Discover Neumarkt's less genteel side at **Grossneumarkt**, where food trucks serve a smorgasbord of multicultural eats. (p67)

Go on a thrifting expedition at Hamburg's best flea market **Flohschanze** (pictured above left), held across hundreds of stalls and graffitied warehouses. The atmosphere is pure St Pauli. (p125)

Devour a *Fischbrötchen* at the **Fischmarkt** (pictured above right) – it's the city's most iconic market experience. For extra points, arrive for the 5am opening after a night out in St Pauli. (p106)

FROM LEFT: KRAFT_STOFF/SHUTTERSTOCK
NOPPASIN WONGCHUM/SHUTTERSTOC

Zum Silbersacke (p124), St Pauli

THE BEST

Historic Drinking Experiences

Rustic *Kneipen* (dive bars) are the cornerstone of Hamburg's drinking culture, with cheap drinks and flexible hours. If their walls could talk, they'd reveal much about the port through its nightlife history.

Visit a basement boxing gym where the People's Champ and Dr Ironfist trained at the Reeperbahn's legendary **Zur Ritze**. (p117)

Sit at the bar of **Gretel & Alfons**, where the Beatles imbibed. The story goes that Paul skipped out once but paid up decades later. (p124)

Discover for yourself what (allegedly) attracted Putin to **Olivia Jones Bar** – a drag show or *Schlager* (German pop), perhaps? Drag queen and celeb Olivia, the owner, might even be here. (p124)

Order the signature caraway shot at **Zum Silbersack**. During the postwar 'Golden Age', hard-partying glitterati and their bouncers drank a lot of 'em. (p124)

Indulge in live jazz at the **Mojo Club**, which appeared in acclaimed German director Fatih Akin's *Soul Kitchen*. (p119)

THE BEST

Shopping Experiences

Shopping could never rival the city's nightlife, but eclectic boutiques and shopping streets deliver just fine, especially when it comes to vintage and handmade pieces. Save luggage space for cool souvenirs.

Stroll St Georg's **Lange Reihe**, where boutique shopping abounds. Giftware and stationery make thoughtful souvenirs. (p78)

Visit elegant arcade **Koppel 66** for arts-and-crafts boutiques and ateliers selling jewellery, ceramics and more. (p79)

Scout out quirky, under-the-radar boutiques like **B.Sweet**, specialising in lingerie and handmade chocolates. (p141)

Pick up the perfect St Pauli FC keepsake, like an LGBTIQ+ rainbow flag or hoodie with the football team's skull-and-crossbones logo (pictured above left) at the **St Pauli-Museum shop**. (p119)

Take home a souvenir – jewellery made from animal bones or West African beadwork – from **Harry's Hamburger Hafenbasar & Museum**. (p95; pictured above right)

Shop cartography treasures at **Dr Götze Land & Karte**, where antique and 3D maps are sure to tickle wanderlust. (p53)

Right: Lange Reihe (p78), St Georg

FROM LEFT: BLICKWINKEL/ALAMY, STEFAN VATER/ALAMY, SCHOENING/ALAMY

THE BEST

Clubbing Experiences

Don't even think of visiting a Hamburg nightclub before midnight. Some don't get going until after 2am. Venues tend to have cover charges; those that don't, play catch-up with expensive drinks.

Get lost in the soundproofed concrete depths of **Uebel & Gefaehrlich**, hidden away in Hamburg's monumental WWII-era bunker. (p111)

Delight in vinyl DJs and punk-scene history in a cosy former smugglers' prison at **Golden Pudel Club**. (p124)

Crowd surf at the Reeperbahn's legendary **Molotow**, where pre-fame headliners have included the Killers and the Black Keys. (p120)

Rave the night away under chandeliers and cherubs on the city's most elegant dance floor, **Docks Prinzenbar**. (p117)

Explore electronic subgenres at **Knust**; once a slaughterhouse, the space now slays experimental music. (p117)

Uebel & Gefaehrlich (p111), St Pauli

Best for Kids

Dip into the world of chocolate at **Chocoversum**, where fun is sprinkled with eco-education and topped by designing your own chocolate bar. (p49)

Gasp at room-sized model worlds at **Miniatur Wunderland**. A 1000m-track model railway (Europe's longest), swooping aeroplanes and Hamburg's active harbour all move in real time. (p88)

Simulate a sailing adventure with a periscope and ogle 50,000 ship models at the **Internationales Maritimes Museum**. (p87)

Tour the 30,000-seat **Millerntor-Stadion** with VIP access to the pitch and lockers; even better, catch an FC St Pauli match there. (p119)

Explore the restored nooks and crannies of 10,000-tonne freighter **Cap San Diego**. Older kids can take on ship-spanning treasure hunts and escape rooms and even climb a high-ropes course. (p122)

Best for Free

Take Europe's longest lift up to the **Elbphilharmonie viewing platform** for 360-degree views across the city. (p90)

Delight in the morning chaos of the Sunday **Fischmarkt**. Rock bands, auctioneering and showboating sellers make for a carnival-like experience. (p106)

Savour some of Hamburg's finest Elbe River views from the green hilltop of **Altonaer Balkon** (Altona Balcony). The locally beloved park offers perfect picnics and scenic walking paths. (p136)

Stroll around the historic boatbuilding village of Oevelgönne, taking in the free open-air **Museumshafen Oevelgönne** harbour museum with its docked restored vessels. (p130)

Trek the 'Mountain Path' at the **Hamburg Bunker**, admiring prime city views and learning WWII history along the way. The panoramic rooftop garden is the ascent's satisfying reward. (p109)

Perfect Days

Central Hamburg's neighbourhoods each have their own individual character and appeal. You can explore them all in just a few days thanks to the city's compact size.

DAY ONE

Only Have One Day?

MORNING

Begin in the Altstadt (old town) with breakfast at **Café Paris** (p52), admiring the **Rathaus** (p38) and **Chilehaus** (p46), before visiting **Mahnmal St Nikolai** (p40; pictured above) for its museum and fabulous views.

AFTERNOON

Wander along picturesque **Deichstrasse** (p47), then have lunch at **Deichgraf** (p47). Walk down to **Landungsbrücken** (p130) for a harbour tour aboard the hop-on, hop-off ferry.

EVENING

Return to Altstadt for a hearty German dinner at **Gröninger Privatbrauerei** (p49), then a classy cocktail at **Le Lion** (p53), live music at **Cascadas** (p50) or a few more beers at **Biergarten Speersort** (p49).

Fischmarkt (p106)

DAY TWO

A Weekend Trip

MORNING
Shop and stroll along the **Lange Reihe** (p78), turning off to visit **Koppel 66** (p79). Head back to the main thoroughfare for brunch at a pavement terrace.

AFTERNOON
Spend an hour or two taking in artisan creations from ancient to Art Nouveau at the **Museum für Kunst und Gewerbe** (p74).

EVENING
Party on the Reeperbahn – it's a rite of passage. The **Grosse Freiheit** (p116; pictured above) strip has the best bar-hopping; catch a **drag show**, **burlesque** or **live music**. Stay up till 5am and hit the **Fischmarkt** (p106) – a *Fischbrötchen* (fish sandwich) is the perfect hangover cure.

DAY THREE

A Short Break

MORNING
Begin with panoramic **Elbphilharmonie** (p89) views: in the early morning, light dances on its glass facades (and you'll miss the crowds).

AFTERNOON
Stroll around Speicherstadt's warehouses and grab lunch on **Deichstrasse** (p47). Walk to the **Mahnmal St Nikolai** (p40) to see its open-air courtyard ruins and take in the UNESCO-recognised **Chilehaus** (p46; pictured above), or visit the world-renowned **Hamburger Kunsthalle** (p43) art museum – allow at least two hours.

EVENING
Take the train to **Lange Reihe** (p78) for eclectic shopping and pre-dinner drinks on a patio. End with happy hour at **Kyti Voo** (p83); it's on from 5pm to 8pm daily.

If You Have More Time

Spend the morning exploring Neustadt's hidden gems. Start with a leisurely stroll along the **Jungfernstieg** (p66) lakeside promenade, then discover the music museums of the **KomponistenQuartier** (p62) and the Baroque wonders of **St Michaelis Kirche** (p58), from the tower to the gargantuan sanctuary and secretive burial crypt.

Grab a fancy multicourse lunch at **Matsumi** (modern Japanese; p68), **Petit Bonheur** (French gastronomy; p68) or **Lusitano** (authentic Portuguese; p68).

Marvel at magnificent archways at the **Alsterarkaden** (p61) and then head over the canal to the **Rathaus** (p38). Join a guided tour through its beehive of rooms (if the timing works out); otherwise, relax in the hidden courtyard by the fountain.

Take the tram to Feldstrasse U-Bahn station and climb to the **Hamburg Bunker's rooftop garden** (p111) for sunset. Grab dinner at **Giovanni Rocco** (p123) and, if you're still buzzing with energy, a few drinks at **St Pauli Eck** (p124).

Alsterarkaden (p61)

PLAN YOUR TRIP PERFECT DAYS

A City Day Trip

Set your course for Hamburg-Altona Station to browse eclectic boutiques in the understatedly cool district of Ottensen. Grab lunch at **Café Mikkels** (p140) or a quick *Fischbrötchen* at **Atlantik Fisch** (p140).

Take the ferry over to Museumhafen Övelgönne; after a 15-minute riverside walk you'll be sunbathing atop soft sands at the **Elbstrand** (p130).

Around sunset, roam around **Övelgönne** (p133), a former fishing and boatbuilding village that's bursting with historic charm. Sailing ships docked in front of the harbour museum make for a gorgeous dusky vista. Hop the 20-minute ferry ride from here back to **St Pauli Piers** (p130; pictured above).

On a Rainy Day

You could easily spend an entire day visiting Speicherstadt's warehouses-turned-museums – besides engaging attractions, many also have lovely canal views. **Miniatur Wunderland** (p88; pictured above) happily guarantees that visitors will lose track of time. The museum rewards an early start: it's a madhouse by afternoon.

Savour Hamburg's maritime history through a unique and immersive sensory visit. Enjoy the scent of roasting beans and fresh brew at **Kaffeemuseum Burg** (p97) or a mix of unusual seasonings at **Spicy's Gewürzmuseum** (p97).

Score last-minute concert tickets to the **Elbphilharmonie** (p89) or another performance venue. Check out EventBrite *(eventbrite.de)*, XCeed *(xceed.me)* and Resident Advisor *(ra.co)*.

21

Get Prepared

BOOK AHEAD

Three months before
Look for hotel deals and book your room. Check out the concert programme at the **Elbphilharmonie** (p89).

One month before
Reserve at Hamburg's most prestigious fine-dining restaurant, **Table** (p100). This is especially true if your visit coincides with a weekend.

One week before
Reserve your spot on guided tours, such as for the **Rathaus** (p38). Buy tickets to skip long queues at **Miniatur Wunderland** (p88).

Manners Matter

Before you take any photos of people (especially children), ask for permission or risk a rebuke.

Keep your voice low in churches and at other historic sites, and respect silent carriages (Ruhewagen/Ruhebereich) on trains.

When parking your bike, leave space for other bike users to lock up. Ride e-scooters in bike lanes and leave the pavement clear for pedestrians when you park.

'Free Entry' at Clubs & Bars

Be wary of 'free entry' at venues on and near St Pauli's Grosse Freiheit and the Reeperbahn; exuberant door staff are tasked with luring in passersby without mentioning that there's a mandatory drink minimum (usually at least €25) once you're inside. Ask at the bar how much drinks cost; you can easily spend €100 for a couple of watered-down cocktails.

Things to Know

Sunday closures Shops and supermarkets in Hamburg tend to close on Sunday; only cafes, some restaurants and a few convenience stores are open. Shops at the Hauptbahnhof (main train station) are the main exception.

Petty crime Watch out for pickpockets, especially around the Reeperbahn and St Pauli after dark. Always lock your bike and never leave your helmet.

Cash While cards are becoming more widely accepted, smaller businesses (kiosks, bakeries and pubs) and market vendors prefer cash. Keep a few euros handy.

Rubbish Littering is strongly frowned upon and can carry fines. If you're staying in an apartment building, separate paper, plastics and general waste into bins or you might hear about it later. Don't throw trash out on Sunday (it's Ruhetag or the 'quiet day').

TIPPING

In Germany, tipping very much reflects the type of establishment and customer satisfaction.

€1–€2 — **Hotels** per day

5–10% — **Restaurants**

Round up — **Bars** to nearest euro

10% — **Taxis**

DAILY BUDGET

Budget: Less than €100

- Hostel or private room: **€20–40**
- Cheap meal: **up to €8**
- Museums: **free–€10**

Midrange: €100–200

- Private apartment or double room: **€60–100**
- Dinner at a nice restaurant: **€50–60**
- Couple of beers in a pub or beer garden: **€8**

Top End: More than €200

- Fancy loft apartment or double in a top-end hotel: **from €150**
- Sit-down lunch and dinner at a top-rated restaurant: **€100**
- Concert or opera tickets: **€20–150**

Currency
euro (€)

Language
German

Time zone
Central European Time (UTC plus one hour)

HAMBURG TOURISMUS GMBH

TIP

The **Hamburg Card** (hamburg.com; 1 day €11.90) offers discounted museum entry, theatre tickets and harbour tours, and free public transport (including harbour ferries). Purchase the card online and read what's covered to get the most value.

When to Go

One of the best things about visiting Hamburg is there's no bad time to go. Hamburgers pay bad weather no mind – their nonchalance is infectious.

Hamburg's weather forecast is a quickly changing mood ring, turning from sunny to *Schmuddelwetter* (grey, rainy, windy) incredibly fast. Despite this, the port city is anything but a fairweather friend to travellers. It's always a good time – and overcast skies even enhance the brooding, maritime scenery. Summer (June-August) is the busiest season, but other times have their definite perks – moderate temps and fewer crowds, for example.

Performing Arts Festivals

April: The **Hamburger Kabarett-Festival** (Hamburg Cabaret Festival; p119) has been high-kicking for more than three decades. The nightly programme, lasting nearly a month and sometimes spilling over into May, is wide-ranging but always a hoot.

June: The three-day **Elbjazz** festival has been going since 2010, featuring shows across its diverse, uniquely atmospheric concert halls and teeny jazz clubs.

August: The **German Burlesque Festival** runs from burlesque to boylesque drag. The inaugural celebration in 2025 was blessed with a visit by the queen of pin-up herself, Dita Von Teese. Off-stage, exhibitions spotlight performance aspects from makeup to costume and choreography.

September: The **Reeperbahn Festival** (p119) takes over Hamburg's famous red-light district in autumn. Across four days, thousands of international visitors

Hamburg

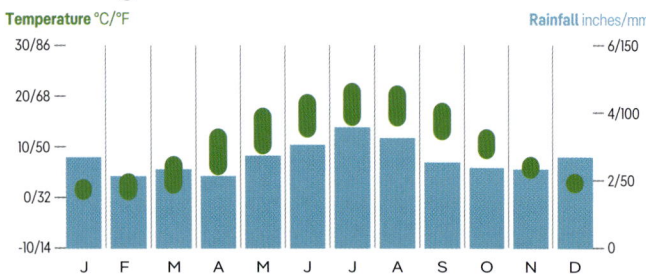

Hamburger Dom (p111)

flock to the city for live music and club performances.

Only in St Pauli

March: Established in 1329, the month-long **Hamburger Dom** (p111) funfair is held three times a year (also in July and November) next to the Hamburg Bunker.

July: **Schlagermove** (p119) celebrates the music genre *Schlager* (mainstream German trash-pop). Everyone dresses up in 1970s fashion to celebrate the German-language disco pop of *Schlager's* original era. The festival takes place across St Pauli from the port area to the Reeperbahn.

September: St Pauli's Spielbudenplatz hosts the **St Pauli Food Truck Festival** (p118) over four or five days in early September and also in mid-May.

November: From mid-November to Christmas Day, Spielbudenplatz becomes the venue for a Reeperbahn appropriate **Christmas Market** (p118) featuring XXX-rated toys, mulled wine, strip shows and 'porno karaoke'.

ACCOMMODATION LOWDOWN

Hamburg has excellent hotels, and standards are generally high across all budgets – even basic accommodation. Reservations are essential between June and September and around major public holidays and festivals. Although it's straightforward to get between neighbourhoods, distances can be great – choose your home base thoughtfully.

✈️ Getting There

Hamburg is well connected by plane and train to the rest of Germany and elsewhere. Most travellers arrive at the city's international airport via Frankfurt, Munich or Berlin.

From the Airport to the City Centre

By Train

The S-Bahn station at Hamburg Airport connects visitors directly to the centre. Take the S1 line (the only line there is) to Hamburg Hauptbahnhof (Central Station), from where there are bus, train and tram connections throughout the city. The S1 arrives every 10 minutes from 5.30am to 1am. The journey from the airport to the Hauptbahnhof takes 25 minutes and costs €3.90.

Buy a ticket at the platform's automated machines or use the app of Hamburg's public transit operator **HVV** *(hvv.de)*.

By Taxi

A taxi from the airport to central Hamburg costs €20 to €30 and takes around 20 minutes (longer, of course, in peak traffic). Taxi queues are outside Terminals 1 and 2.

By Rideshare

Hamburg authorities have cracked down hard on ridesharing services. You likely won't find a pick-up on demand, though you could try reserving ahead.

Other Points of Entry

Central Station

Hamburg Hauptbahnhof is the city's main transport hub, receiving direct, high-speed Deutsche Bahn services from Berlin (two hours), Cologne (four hours), Frankfurt (3½ hours) and Munich (5¾ to seven hours). A direct service to Copenhagen (Denmark; five to six hours) runs several times daily.

FlixTrain has direct routes from Berlin and Frankfurt to Hamburg (the trains are significantly slower: three hours and 7½ hours respectively).

> **Hamburg Cruise Center Altona**
>
> Hamburg is a popular port for cruise ships. There are no international ferry services to Hamburg; the nearest departures are from Kiel.

Getting Around

For the avid *Spaziergänger* (walker), Hamburg is a dream. Walking is the best mode of sightseeing and your feet will get you around the city centre just fine. A Hamburg Card, which includes unlimited public transport, is a worthwhile investment, though. It's excellent value for exploring less-visited areas – and your calf muscles will thank you.

Walking

Downtown Hamburg might be compact, but the city's expansive residential areas are also well worth exploring. Stroll strategically, especially if you plan to visit a few museums too. The excellent public transportation system can save you much time and energy, especially at the end of a long day.

Bikes & E-Scooters

Download the **StadtRad Hamburg app** *(stadtradhamburg.de)* and pick up a bright-red seven-gear bike from one of the docking stations. The first 30 minutes of every ride are free; after that it's €0.10 per minute or €24 per day. Bikes are allowed free of charge aboard S-/U-Bahn trains and buses on weekends and outside peak weekday hours (6am to 9am and 4pm to 6pm) and on ferries any time.

Pay-per-use e-scooters are available around the city, but beware the abundant no-parking zones (indicated by red areas in the app) where you can't end your ride. E-scooters must be parked legally (not blocking pavements); the city can remove them and you'll be fined on the app.

ABOVE: MANUEL J. SACHSE/SHUTTERSTOCK
BELOW: WERNER SPREMBERG/SHUTTERSTOCK

--- ESSENTIAL APP ---

Download the **HVV** *(hvv.de)* app for the most up-to-date route planning and paperless tickets.

Rental Cars & Car Sharing

Driving around Hamburg is easy: thoroughfares are well signposted (though watch for one-way streets in the centre) and parking stations plentiful. Most inner-city parking stations charge around €4 per hour or €28 per day. Ask if your hotel has private or discounted parking. On-street parking usually has a two-hour limit.

Consider signing up for car-sharing apps (Cambio, Greenwheels, Flinkster), where you pay per ride by distance or minute. For these you'll need to get your driver's licence verified before you travel – you might need an international licence to do so. Cambio vehicles often have children's car seats; otherwise, you'll need your own.

Taxi & Uber

Hamburg's cream-coloured taxis are easy to find. Keep Taxi Hamburg's number handy: 040-666 666. Due to local regulation, Uber vehicles are limited.

Public Transport

HVV operates Hamburg's entire public transport system: U-Bahn and S-Bahn trains, trams, buses and commuter ferries. A single-trip ticket can be used for a continuous journey of up to 120 minutes after validation; you can switch routes within two hours, but you can't use the same single ticket to go back. Stamp your ticket at an orange ticket validator before boarding.

Public Transport Essentials

Trains & Trams

The frequent U-Bahn (four lines) and S-Bahn (six lines) trains are easily the best way to get around the city. They're always easy to figure out, and if you're unsure just ask another passenger.

There's little difference between the U-Bahn and S-Bahn, though U-Bahn trains are generally more frequent, running every two to 10 minutes as against the S-Bahn's frequency of every 10 to 20 minutes. U-Bahn and S-Bahn lines frequently intersect. The U-Bahn and S-Bahn will get you between neighbourhoods; trams are most handy for travelling shorter distances and saving some walking around downtown.

Buses

Public buses cover the city but can be confusing unless you know where you're going.

Ferries

The commuter ferry system is an excellent way to cover the riverside, and a much cheaper (and more authentic) alternative to the tourist-oriented harbour cruises.

The cost is a standard single-journey HVV ticket. Ferries operate all along the Elbe River and between HafenCity and Altona.

Operating Hours & Peak Times

Bus and rail services run from 4am to midnight during the week and around the clock on weekends and the night before a public holiday. From 12.30am to 4am Sunday to Thursday less frequent night buses take over (frankly, you might as well call a taxi). Ferries run from 5.30am to 11.15pm, generally every 15 minutes.

There's a morning rush before 9.30am and from 4.30pm to 6.30pm. On weekends, transport tends to be a little less crowded, though ferries are still popular for sightseeing.

TRAVEL COSTS

Single-journey ticket
€3.90

Adult day pass
€7.80

One-day Hamburg Card with unlimited public transport
€11.90

HAMBURG CARD

The **Hamburg Card** *(hamburg.com)* includes unlimited public transport; also covering some attractions, it's good value.

TICKETS

Train tickets must be purchased from machines at stations; bus tickets are available from the driver. Purchasing them via the app (or, even better, getting a day pass) saves time. Queues at ticket machines get long, especially at peak times and at busier stations (Reeperbahn, Hauptbahnhof).

There are no turnstiles at train stations. Inspectors conduct random checks on board and issue fines. Train tickets are the same as those for bus and U-/S-Bahn services and can be purchased at vending machines at most stops.

TICKET ZONES

The city is divided into zones. Ring A covers the centre, inner suburbs and airport. Ticket machines and the app automatically input the correct zone when you enter the stations you're travelling between.

🎁 A Few Surprises

Germany's largest port is famous for its warehouses, but there's plenty more to Hamburg beyond its serious mercantile history.

Craft Breweries

Hamburg is home to one of Europe's busiest, most experimental and highly collaborative **craft-brewing scenes** (p138). Seek out the sprawling warehouse production facilities of various makers – find them tucked into residential areas outside the centre – and drop in for brewery tours and tastings at brewpubs.

Head to **Wildwuchs Brauwerk**, the first certified organic brewery in Germany, in Hamburg's growing sustainable district, Wilhelmsburg (p58). Another scene favourite, **Landgang Brauerei**, has a taproom made out of shipping containers. Dining at **Altes Mädchen** (p138) restaurant in the Schanzenviertel is a unique gourmand's experience with craft brew pairings to your dishes and preferences selected by an in-house beer sommelier.

Underground Clubbing

Hamburg's nightlife scene spans an eclectic range of underground venues with fascinating former lives. Among the reincarnated are warehouses flipped into nightclubs (techno temples **NCTS** and **Südpol** are standouts) and concert halls converted from factories: **Knust** (p117) was a slaughterhouse, **Fabrik** (p139) a manufacturing plant. Nightlife's karmic cycle isn't all industrial, though: there's **Docks Prinzenbar** (p117), a Baroque theatre now home to Hamburg's most beautiful dance floor, the vinyl DJ institution **Golden Pudel Club** (p124) in a former smugglers' prison; and former pet store **Hijack**, reborn as a party-hardy club-art gallery.

The most evocative clubbing experiences, though, are surely dancing to heavy bass lines in a WWII bunker at **Uebel &**

OFFBEAT HAMBURG

Feast your eyes on peculiar objects from a sailor's travels at **Harry's Hamburger Hafenbasar & Museum** (p95).

Dine on traditional Hamburg cuisine in the bridge-nestled **Oberhafen Kantine** (Port Cantine; p96).

Climb high ropes aboard the **Cap San Diego** (p122), a historic freighter moored on the Elbe River.

Go for a dinner-time dance on docked party boat **Frau Hedi** (p121), where disco reigns supreme.

Altonaer Balkon (p136)

Gefaehrlich (p111) and headbanging to metal and psychedelic funk in the 1964-built East German fishing vessel **MS Stubnitz**.

Freaky & Geeky

Hamburg's history of maritime trade, and thus global ideas and technology, has spawned a couple of museums devoted to the weirder side of science.

The **Deutsches Zusatzstoffmuseum** (German Food Additives Museum; p98) sheds light on additives in the food industry. Meanwhile, the **Medizinhistorisches Museum** (Medical History Museum; p98), in Hamburg's University Teaching Hospital, keeps a peculiar treasure trove of historical medical instruments. Stethoscopes, eerie wax figures and more trace the evolution of hospital care from the 19th century to the present.

Unexpected Greenery

Hamburg's not all shoreline and shipping vessels. Seeking out the port city's underrated green spaces can be a truly calming experience. Grassy expanses offer a range of scenery and vibes. Waterside greens go quirky at St Pauli's locally beloved **Park Fiction** (p122); its plastic palm trees and 'flying carpet' lawn were designed by residents. Meanwhile, on the **Altonaer Balkon** (p136) you'll get a different harbour perspective from panoramic, hilltop heights. In construction-heavy HafenCity, **Baakenpark** (p98) offers an airy escape from sightseeing crowds.

Explore Hamburg

Altstadt	35
Neustadt	55
St Georg	71
Speicherstadt & HafenCity	85
St Pauli & the Reeperbahn	103
Altona & the Elbmeile	127

Hamburg's Walking Tours

Hamburg's Historic Heart	44
Notably Neustadt	64
St Georg: Alternative & Arty	76
Where Speicherstadt Meets HafenCity	92
St Pauli by Day	112
St Pauli by Night	114
Ottensen: Hamburg's Quiet Achiever	134

Elbmeile (p130)
JAN HENDRIK/SHUTTERSTOCK

See p52 for eating, drinking and shopping listings

Explore
Altstadt

Studded with architectural landmarks, including impressive maritime facades largely rebuilt following WWII destruction, Altstadt is Hamburg's historic heart. It's also a modern city hub you'll come through again and again. Even better, the neighbourhood delivers a truly authentic slice of local life: unlike in many other German old town centres, there's much to enjoy after the sightseeing is done. The historic merchants quarter eschews ye olde downtown tourist traps and offers appealing cafes, atmospheric beer taverns and eating options for a range of budgets. Give yourself at least one full day to roam around.

Getting Around

Walking
Altstadt is compact enough to explore on foot. Start this way and then switch to public transport once your legs have had enough. Chilehaus is a 10-minute walk from Hamburg Hauptbahnhof.

Public Transport
The neighbourhood is well connected to the rest of the city by U-Bahn, S-Bahn and tram. A block south of Chilehaus is the U-Bahn station Messberg.

Biking
Cycling is a convenient option, aside from the odd cobblestone street.

Chilehaus (p46)
TALJAT DAVID/SHUTTERSTOCK

THE BEST

ENIGMATIC CITY HALL
Rathaus (p38)

UNESCO ARCHITECTURE
Chilehaus (p46)

FAMOUS ART MUSEUM
Hamburger Kunsthalle (p43)

WAR-RAVAGED CHURCH
Mahnmal St Nikolai (p40)

OLD MERCHANTS QUARTER
Deichstrasse (p46)

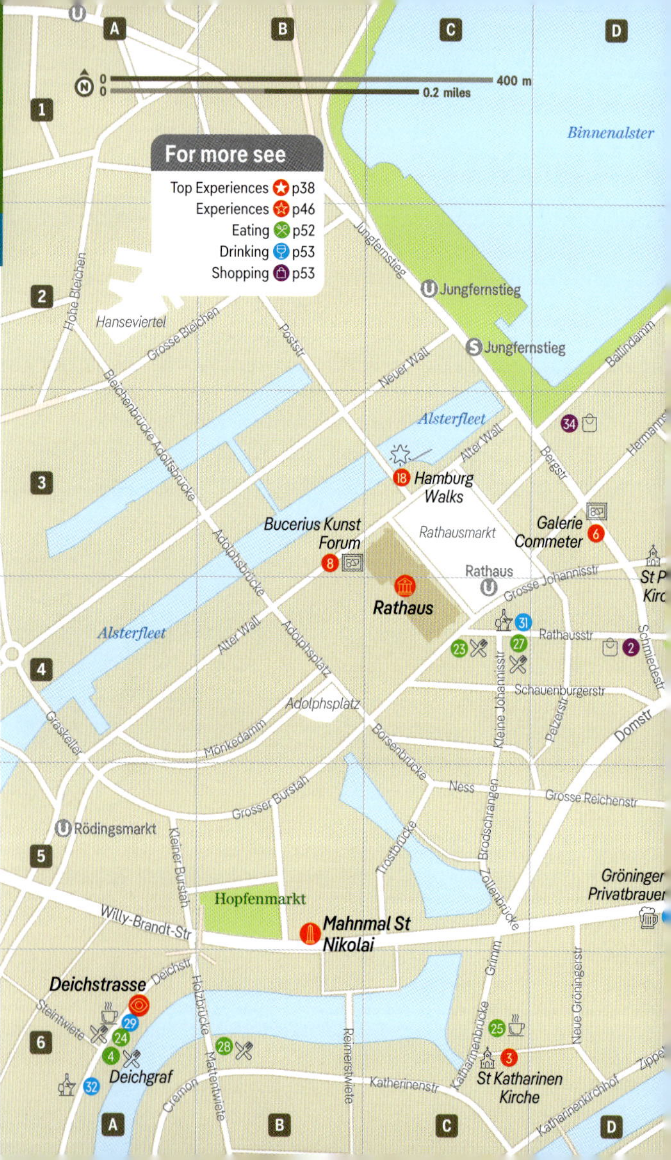

ALTSTADT

For more see

- Top Experiences ⭐ p38
- Experiences 🌸 p46
- Eating 🟢 p52
- Drinking 🔵 p53
- Shopping 🟣 p53

Binnenalster

Ⓤ Jungfernstieg
Ⓢ Jungfernstieg

Alsterfleet

Hamburg Walks 18

Bucerius Kunst Forum 8

Rathausmarkt

Rathaus

Galerie Commeter 6

St P Kirc

23 · 31 · 27 Rathausstr

Alsterfleet

Adolphsplatz

2

Ⓤ Rödingsmarkt

Hopfenmarkt

Mahnmal St Nikolai

Gröninger Privatbrauer

Deichstrasse

29 · 24

Deichgraf 4

32 · 28

25

St Katharinen Kirche 3

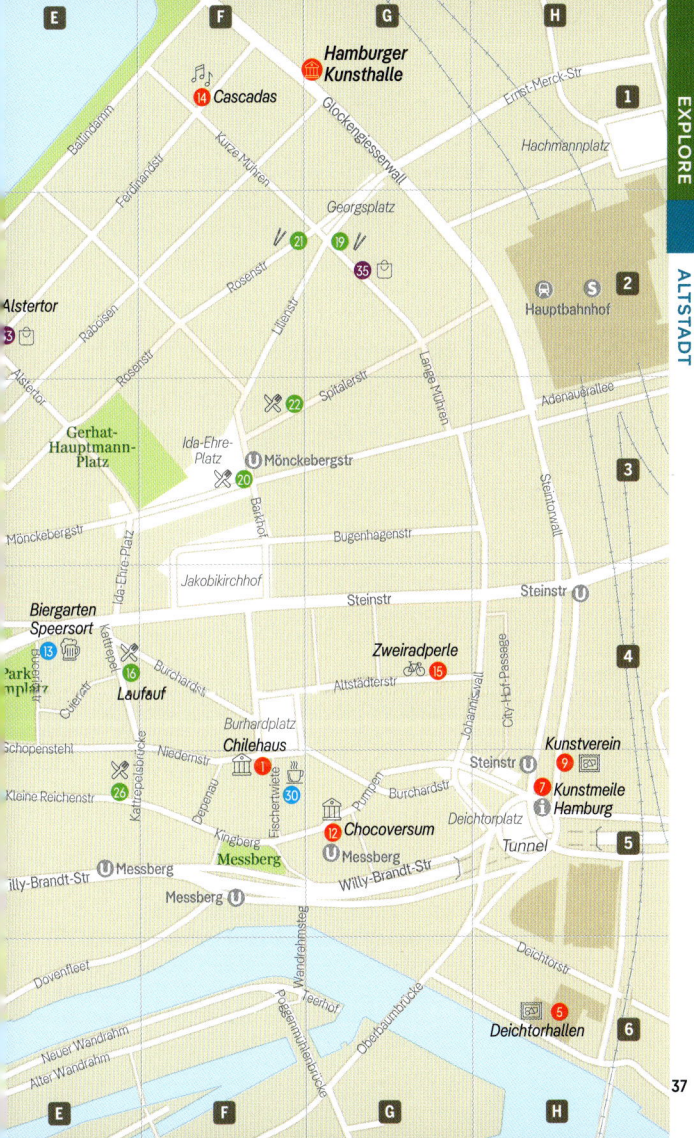

⭐ TOP EXPERIENCE

Rathaus

Hamburg's 1897 **Rathaus** (City Hall) is a palatial neo-Renaissance beehive of indoor and outdoor gems. The airy 'hidden' courtyard is one of the city's most wonderful places to unwind. Guided tours weave between grand labyrinthine rooms, some still used for governance today.

MAP P36 **C4**

PLANNING TIP
By late afternoon or early evening, try to position yourself along the waterfront. Locals and fellow travellers catching boats against the floodlit Rathaus are a memorable sight.

Architecture, History & Tours

Like much of Hamburg's inner city, the Rathaus was devastated in the Great Fire of 1842. The current City Hall, rebuilt in the late 19th century, is very different from its modest medieval predecessor. An ornate, neo-Renaissance style was considered to be well suited to the neighbouring buildings in Neustadt and emblematic of a prosperous port.

Crowned by a 112m-high tower, the facade is especially beautiful for its balcony, where Hammonia, Hamburg's patron goddess, and the city's coat of arms are depicted. The main entrance includes an elaborate wrought-iron gate and a roof supported by sandstone columns.

Tours wind through the most renowned of the Rathaus' maze of 647 rooms. See the city's official website *(hamburg.de)* for information on specified days for tours in English, which run at 11.15am, 1.15pm and 3.15pm. Tours in German take place daily, usually every half hour (less frequently from November to March).

Grand Entrance Hall & Courtyard

The **Grand Entrance Hall** features 16 imposing granite columns, each carved from a different type of stone found across the German Empire. They frame floor and mosaic murals commemorating national unity and Hanseatic League seafaring history.

Scan this QR code to book a guided tour.

SAIKO3P/SHUTTERSTOCK

Walk through the Grand Entrance Hall into the palatial inner courtyard, free for public entry. Tables and comfy chairs overlook a fountain ornamented by a bronze figure of Hygieia, the Greek goddess of health. She commemorates Germany's last major cholera epidemic in 1892.

Ceremonial Rooms

Tours visit the **Emperor's Hall** (Kaisersaal), named to commemorate a visit by Kaiser Wilhelm II in 1895. The adjacent Tower Hall is still used for ceremonies.

The pinnacle of the Rathaus' splendour is the nearly 50m-long **Grand Ballroom**. Vast paintings here recount 1200 years of Hamburg history.

You can visit active government rooms such as the Senate chamber (there are no windows, only a glass room – by German custom, councils only meet in open air) and sign the Golden Book in the Mayor's Hall.

QUICK BREAK
Elegant **Café Paris** (cafeparis. net; p52), a *Jugendstil* (Art Nouveau) stunner, is a fitting stop for coffee or a meal. It's good at any time of the day, but brunch is its strongest suit.

★ TOP EXPERIENCE

Mahnmal St Nikolai

At once haunting and soaring, this half ruin is a distinct sight that includes a war memorial and an observation tower boasting some of Hamburg's most striking views. This combination of sobering history and an uplifting experience gives **Mahnmal St Nikolai** (Memorial of St Nicholas) particular impact.

MAP P36 **B5**

PLANNING TIP
Arrive as close to opening time as you can – the queues can be long throughout the day, and only so many people can fit in the elevator at once.

Scan this QR code for info on events such as carillon concerts.

Architecture & History

Once Hamburg's tallest and most magnificent Gothic Revival church, St Nikolai was built over decades from 1195. In 1943, in minutes, it was reduced to rubble by Allied bombardment. The onslaught and resultant firestorm destroyed all but the church tower. Difficult as it is to imagine now, St Nikolai was the world's tallest building from 1874 to 1876. Even today it remains the city's second-tallest structure (after the TV tower that you can see on the horizon away to the north – though that structure is closed to the public). What remains at the site is at once magnificent and profoundly moving.

Great Glass Elevator

The highlight for many visitors is the **glass lift** up to a 76.3m-high viewing platform inside the surviving spire that offers a panorama of Hamburg's centre.

Views from here are all-encompassing and utterly breathtaking. From up high, the port's watery personality is fully apparent, and the view of the harbour – all ships and silhouettes – is offset by

SERGEYPHOTO7/SHUTTERSTOCK

the epoch-defining Elbphilharmonie (p89), which is very difficult to take your eyes off. If you're keen to see Hamburg at its best, visit as close to sunset as the opening hours allow to see the city bathed in golden light.

The slender, octagonal spire is the last surviving remnant of St Nikolai. The structure's ornate neo-Gothic flying buttresses and pointed arches pay tribute to French cathedrals. The open belfry allows views through the tower, though its bell is permanently silent, to commemorate victims of war.

Crypt Museum

The **crypt**, just to one side of the concourse (which was once the church's main sanctuary), houses an unflinching underground exhibit on the horrors of war. The basement museum's

QUICK BREAK
Cross the main road (Willy Brandt Strasse) to **Deichstrasse** (p47). This preserved part of the former merchants quarter has plentiful gastronomy options.

UWE ARANAS/SHUTTERSTOCK

OPERATION GOMORRAH
Over eight days and seven nights in 1943, Operation Gomorrah saw much of Hamburg's city centre, including the church of St Nikolai, incinerated. The bombing, a combined offensive by the British and Americans, targeted the port city because it was an important ship-building location. A massive firestorm killed at least 35,000, left one million homeless and wrecked Hamburg's economy for many years following.

exhibition focuses on three events in WWII: the German bombing of Coventry in 1940; the German destruction of Warsaw in 1944; and Operation Gomorrah, the combined British and American bombing of Hamburg in 1943.

Courtyard Ruins

The church's **courtyard ruins** also present a stark contrast to the observation deck's heartlifting experience. Walking around walls of rubble and collapsed arches – remnants of the cathedral's vaulting, preserved after the bombing rather than rebuilt – firmly ground the landmark in its present-day function as a war memorial (pictured above). Even if you don't pay to go up the observation tower you can visit the courtyard, where there are free, changing exhibitions of war photography and social art.

⭐ TOP EXPERIENCE

Hamburger Kunsthalle

Hamburg's most prestigious art gallery, the **Hamburger Kunsthalle** *(hamburger-kunsthalle.de; adult/child €16/free)* is also one of Germany's best art spaces.

MAP P36 **G1**

Old Masters & 19th Century

The museum's chronological starting point has its most venerable works. Amid the numerous examples of religious triptychs and other sacred German pieces, some European names stand out: Lucas Cranach the Younger, Francisco José de Goya y Lucientes and Peter Paul Rubens.

Some of the weightiest names from 19th-century European art are represented here too. Again, they're a pretty international lot: Edgar Degas, Caspar David Friedrich, Max Liebermann, Édouard Manet, Claude Monet and Auguste Rodin. Highlights include Paul Gauguin's *Breton Boys Bathing* and Friedrich's *Wanderer above the Sea of Fog*.

Classical Modernism

This gallery is devoted to the late 19th and early 20th centuries up to the 1970s, a period distinguished by a break with tradition. The elite group whose work is shown here includes Francis Bacon, Max Ernst, Paul Klee, Edvard Munch and Pablo Picasso. Munch's *Madonna* and Klee's *Revolution of the Viaduct* exemplify the gallery's diverse styles.

Gegenwart & Contemporary Art

The museum's contemporary art collection finds its own perfect home in the separate, cube-like Galerie der Gegenwart. It houses works by Gerhard Richter (considered Germany's greatest living artist) as well as international stars including Jeff Koons and Andy Warhol.

PLANNING TIP

Don't plan to visit the gallery on a Monday (it's closed). The museum stays open later on Thursday nights and is cheaper but more crowded.

Scan this QR code for info on current exhibitions.

WALKING TOUR

Hamburg's Historic Heart

In Altstadt the full range of Hamburg's architectural eras come together seamlessly. With a lively contemporary beat, the city's historic heart is also a place where hallmarks of the past are preserved and fittingly celebrated. Stroll across hundreds of years of the port city's history, taking in realms from food to construction along the way.

START	END	LENGTH
Chilehaus	Gröninger Privatbrauerei	450m; 30 minutes

1 Ship-shaped Beauty

Stand between the A and B buildings of the **Chilehaus** (p46) for the best vantage point on this UNESCO World Heritage Site. From here you can easily pick out the 1924 Gothic brick structure's ship-like shape – a stunning example of what's left of Hamburg's Kontorhaus (merchant commerce) District. Note that the commercial spaces inside can't be visited but they're not worth the time anyway – big, industrial expanses for combining work and storage are, these days, better suited to medical offices and agencies.

2 Seat of Power

Make your way to Hamburg's **Rathaus** (p38), where you can take in its striking Grand Entrance Hall and – perhaps its finest feature – an open-air courtyard with plenty of public seating. Throw some change in goddess Hygieia's fountain for luck and watch dolled-up brides and grooms pose for wedding photos. The best times to visit are early morning, when the facade is bathed in golden light, or after sunset for a moody long-exposure shot.

3 Brasserie Stop

Within a spectacularly tiled 1882 butchers hall and adjoining Art Deco salon, the elegant yet relaxed **Café Paris** (p52) serves excellent brasserie classics such as croque-monsieur and steak tartare. Of course, it's also divine for an expertly made café au lait.

4 Ruined Church

Once the world's tallest building, the **Mahnmal St Nikolai** (Memorial of St Nicholas; p40) is now a ruin whose last surviving relic is its tower spire. Even if you don't go up to the observation deck (though you should) or visit the crypt museum, be sure to walk through the front entrance and past the lift into the open-air courtyard, where free special exhibits are staged next to the rubble.

5 Old Merchants District

Wander up and down **Deichstrasse** (p47), where restored 18th-century homes reveal the old canal and merchants district. Now there's excellent food to be found here, including Nord Coast Coffee Roasters (p53) and one of Hamburg's best restaurants, Deichgraf (p47).

6 Historic Beer Hall

The perfect finish to this walk is sliding into a communal table at one of the city's oldest breweries. Take an invigorating sip of 200 years of beer-making history at **Gröninger Privatbrauerei** (p49). Traditional German fare makes up its hearty menu.

EXPERIENCES

Marvel at Chilehaus MARITIME ARCHITECTURE

MAP: ❶ P36 **F5**

One of Hamburg's most beautiful buildings is the **Chilehaus**. The crowning gem of the UNESCO-anointed merchant commerce Kontorhaus District (p47), she's a brick-and-copper beauty. Shaped like an ocean liner, the building features remarkable curved walls like a ship's bow and staggered balconies reminiscent of decks. It was designed by architect Fritz Höger for a merchant who derived his wealth from trading with Chile. Casual visitors are not really welcome inside (today's renters are mainly private offices), but it's the exterior you really come here to see.

Grab a cappuccino at Palang Good Coffee (p53), between Chilehaus' A and B buildings, and circle around the edifice.

If you stand at the corner of Fischertwiete and Pumpengasse you'll get the best straight-on view of the building's ship-like silhouette.

Score Hamburg Football Memorabilia TEAM MERCH

Football fans can pick up jerseys, hats and other fan memorabilia of Hamburg's most successful soccer team, Hamburger SV or HSV (Kevin Keegan played here in the 1970s), at **Hamburger SV City StorE** (MAP: ❷ P36 **D4**). The Altstadt flagship store has everything with the HSV logo you can imagine and even more. It's closed Sunday.

Go Inside a Pirate's Church MARITIME SANCTUARY

With swooping white exposed-brick walls, snowy stained glass and a sky-high 29m nave, the inside of **St Katharinen Kirche** (MAP: ❸ P36 **C6**; *katharinen-hamburg.de; free*) looks exactly like a misty sea morning. It's easy to see why the church was known for welcoming seamen. Legend also says it was built upon pirate's treasure. After a 12-year restoration completed in 2019, the church looks sparkling new. Besides the nave, gorgeous highlights include a glimmering, sunlit organ once played by Johann Sebastian Bach and golden ornaments said to have belonged to the legendary pirate Klaus Störtebeker.

A less prominent side entrance to St Catherine's lies on the quiet Grimm. After your visit, have dinner under the church's imposing shadow at the adjacent Nardo's (p52).

Stroll the Merchants Quarter NOSTALGIC ARCHITECTURE

Hamburg's Great Fire of 1842 broke out on **Deichstrasse** (MAP: P36 **A6**), which features a few restored 18th-century homes, most now housing restaurants. You can get a real feel for the old canal and merchants quarter here, thanks to the buildings' old-world appearance.

There are several good eating options on Deichstrasse, but none will give you a more atmospheric feeling of historic Altstadt than **Deichgraf** (MAP: ❹ P36 **A6**; *deichgraf-hamburg.de*). A Hamburg institution, and considered one of the city's best restaurants, Deichgraf excels in regional specialities cooked to a high standard. The menu changes seasonally, and much of the food is sourced from the region. Its *Labskaus* (a savoury northern delicacy of meat, fish and potato stew) is especially good, and it even offers a smaller portion for those who just want a taste. The prime setting – water on one side and long, street-fronting tables on the other – adds to its charm. Deichgraf is closed Sunday and Monday.

Visit an Industrial Art Gallery ART AND PHOTOGRAPHY
MAP: ❺ P36 **H6**

Deichtorhallen *(deichtorhallen. de; adult/child €13/free, closed Mon)* is composed of two grandly restored brick market halls, built in 1911 and 1913 respectively, that are home to high-profile special exhibitions of modern art and photography. The main **Haus der Photographie** (Hall for Contemporary Photography) is closed for extensive renovation until 2026, and in the meantime photography exhibitions are held in Phoxxi, a shipping container with an eye-catching multi-coloured design by Berlin-based artist Anselm Reyle.

The expansive grounds, **Phoxxi Green Area**, include a bar and are also increasingly used for open-air electronic-music parties on the grounds surrounding the south and eastern side of the buildings. Check **Xceed** *(xceed. me)* for schedules and tickets.

 KONTORHAUS DISTRICT

Hamburg's UNESCO-listed Kontorhaus District was once the port's beating business heart. The compact merchant commerce district, lying between Steinstrasse, Burchardstrasse, Johanniswall and Klosterwall, is packed with *Kontore* (traditional office buildings used by merchants and trading companies during the late 19th and early 20th centuries). Unlike residential buildings, every *Kontor* was a state-of-the-art example of function meets form. They were purpose built, combining sprawling office and storage space, always with an artistic touch. Hamburg's Kontorhaus District, mostly built in the 1920s, is one of the best-preserved examples of northern Germany's unique *Kontor* architectural style: practical brick construction with expressionist flourishes.

ART MILE

Hamburg's five-pack of renowned art institutions, known as the **Kunstmeile** (Art Mile; MAP: 7 P36 H5), will excite any art lover. With a three-day Art Mile Pass from the official **website** *(kunstmeile-hamburg.de; 3-day ticket €35)* you can feast your eyes on them all. Beyond the world-renowned **Hamburger Kunsthalle** (p43), industrial art hall **Deichtorhallen** (p47) and Europe's foremost applied-arts institution, the **Museum für Kunst und Gewerbe** (p74), the ticket includes admission to two more institutions: **Bucerius Kunst Forum** (MAP: 8 P36 B3), a private museum focused on socially conscious multimedia art, and **Kunstverein** (MAP: 9 P36 H5), a local art association for emerging contemporary artists.

Enjoy Free Modern Art   HAMBURG'S OLDEST GALLERY

Founded in 1821, privately run **Galerie Commeter** (MAP: 6 P36 D3; *commeter.de; free, closed Sun & Mon*) is a Hamburg institution – but it's by no means conservative. Its shipshape interiors showcase thoroughly modern works. Take in a reliable offering of contemporary European painting, graphics, sculpture and photography.

Hamburg's Oldest Parish   CHURCH AND PANORAMA

Just around the corner from the Rathaus, **St Petri Kirche** (MAP: 10 P36 D3; *sankt-petri.de; St Peter's Church; tower adult/child €5/free*) is Hamburg's oldest parish, with roots going back to the 12th century (though the building itself did not survive the Great Fire of 1842 and was reconstructed afterwards). The bronze lion-head door handles (on display but not currently functioning) date back to 1340 and, having survived the Great Fire, are among the city's oldest art relics.

With little fanfare, St Petri is home to Hamburg's highest accessible **viewing platform**. Climb the 544 steps of the church's 123m-tall spire and be treated to a stunning panorama through the tower portholes – across the city centre and, on a clear day, all the way to the port.

Drink in a German Beer Hall   HISTORIC BREWERY

Down in the cellar of one of Hamburg's oldest breweries and beer halls, take a sip of famous pils tapped from old oak barrels. **Gröninger Privatbrauerei** (MAP: 11 P36 D5; *groeninger-hamburg.de, closed Sun & Mon*) is Hamburg's most atmospheric traditional beer hall – a vision of classic wood-panelled decor, long communal tables and vintage 19th-century brewery equipment under vaulted ceilings.

A variety of classic beers are made according to the German *Reinheitsgebot* (Beer Purity Law) of 1516, a formula that, for the most part, Hamburg and its countless craft breweries choose to abstain from.

Besides the lager and malty *Dunkel* pours, ordering the pork knuckles served with crackling is always an excellent decision.

Make Your Own Chocolate at Chocoversum CHOCOLATE MUSEUM
MAP: 12 P36 G5

Who needs an excuse to fall in love with chocolate? At the fun **Chocoversum** *(chocoversum.de; tours adult/child €29/15)* you can dive into the world of sustainable chocolate on a 90-minute guided tour. Interactive exhibits and displays paint a rich picture of the economic conditions behind chocolate's supply chain, from the working conditions on cacao farms to the importance of ethically sourcing beans. At the end, during the hands-on chocolate-making experience, you have the chance to design your own chocolate bar, from the type of chocolate used to the toppings and wrapper.

Savour a Bavarian Beer Garden TRADITIONAL RESTAURANT

There's nothing very complicated about **Biergarten Speersort** (MAP: 13 P36 E4) a Bavarian-style beer garden overlooking one of the few open green spaces in Hamburg's centre. The outdoor tables are simply a wonderful place to drink beer on a sunny day. If your visit to Germany doesn't include going down south, this is the perfect place to drink Höfbrau lager from a *mass* (1L beer mug) one-handed and indulge in Bavarian delicacies such as cheesy *Spätzle* (egg noodles) and saucy *Maultaschen* (Germany's answer to ravioli).

  FIVE PROTESTANT CHURCHES

Hamburg was an early and enthusiastic adopter of the Protestant Reformation and Martin Luther's 16th-century theology. By 1529, 12 years after Luther's *Ninety-Five Theses,* the city had officially become Lutheran. Today Hamburg shepherds a flock of five prominent Protestant churches. In addition to St Petri, St Katharinen (p46) and St Nikolai (p40) there are St Jacobi and St Michaelis (p58). These sanctuaries all lie in the city centre within a roughly 2km radius of each other that's easily covered by foot in an afternoon. St Nikolai, now a war memorial, is the only one that no longer holds services.

Dance to Latin Rhythms
LIVE MUSIC

One of the better live music venues outside St Pauli (p103), **Cascadas** (MAP: 14 P36 F1; *cascadas.club; hours vary*) offers up a nightly programme that ranges across soul, jazz, Latin, funk, Caribbean and blues. Things usually get going around 8pm, but check the website for upcoming gigs and times – buy your tickets online to avoid needless queuing. Admission prices depend on the event but are usually €5 to €20.

Cycle Around Altstadt
BIKE SHOP

Visit **Zweiradperle** (MAP: 15 P36 G4; *zweiradperle.hamburg*) and pick up your own wheels to explore the Altstadt – let's face it, an e-bike is a splendid means of getting around, especially after racking up plenty of steps in the museums. The shop offers a range of rental bikes *(from €19 per day, including helmets and locks)* as well as tours – the three-hour tour *(€36)* is a great introduction to the city. All tours start at the shop, where you'll also find a cool cafe to fuel up in before you hit the road.

Eat a Labskaus at Laufauf
NORTHERN GERMAN FARE

MAP: 16 P36 E4

A bastion for northern German and Hamburg cooking, **Laufauf** *(laufauf.de, closed Sun)* is something of an institution. It's a pretty casual place that gets a mostly local crowd.

Consider this your dining safe haven to try some of northern Germany's favourite dishes, reliably cooked to perfection. *Hamburger pannfisch* (fried local fish), *Bratheringe* (fried herring) and *Matjesfilet* (herring fillet) are all

---

PATCHWORK CITYSCAPE

Harmonising surviving prewar structures, functionalist feats and seafaring motifs, Hamburg's architecture is a fascinating mishmash. The city centre of mostly Gothic and neo-Gothic architecture was destroyed in WWII. The Rathaus (p38) and St Michaelis Kirche (p58) remain as two old-world (neo-Renaissance and Baroque) icons, while 19th-century Speicherstadt (p85) highlights a Gothic Revival influence. Mid-20th-century functionalism saw classic architecture razed for unappealing utilitarian structures. The period's 'high point' is the Fernsehturm (TV Tower), still Hamburg's tallest building. These days architects are keenly incorporating ultra-contemporary maritime motifs along the harbour, among them the Elbphilharmonie (p89) and Dockland (p131).

orders you can't go wrong with, but for true local immersion you must order the *labskaus* (a meat, fish and potato stew with beetroot). *Labskaus* is the port city's most beloved homegrown dish, and you really can't knock it till you try it.

Climb Hamburg's Prettiest Staircase   KONTOR ARCHITECTURE

The 1900-built, clinker-brick **Alstertor** (MAP: 17 P36 E2), often referred to as the *Heintzehof*, is a fine example of northern German *Kontor* design. It's worth a peek inside for a lesser-known attraction: a striking three-quarter spiral staircase deemed by locals to be one of Hamburg's loveliest architectural features.

Take a photograph, preferably with a wide-angle setting, from the ground floor looking up to capture the sweeping combination of wooden railings, stone steps and large windows in aesthetic harmony. The best lighting arrives just before sunset.

The impressive travel bookstore Dr Götze Land & Karte (p53) is also located inside the building.

Take a Walking Tour of Altstadt   GUIDED EXPERIENCE

Hamburg Walks (MAP: 18 P36 C3; hamburgwalks.de) offers a 2½ hour **Discover Hamburg tour** *(€20 per person),* which mostly focuses on Altstadt. The Kontorhaus District (p47), Mahnmal St Nikolai (p40) and the Rathaus (p38) are all covered, and the tour has plenty of historical detail and local colour.

BEST FREE SIGHTSEEING

Rathaus
MAP: P36 C4
Walk through the City Hall's lobby to the open-air courtyard. Pull up a seat at free public tables and people-watch around the fountain – it's popular for wedding photo shoots. (p38)

Mahnmal St Nikolai
MAP: P36 B5
The courtyard ruins are free to enter and hold socially conscious exhibitions on war and its aftermath; these often take the form of documentary photography and art installations. (p40)

Galerie Commeter
MAP: 6 P36 D3
Established in 1821, Hamburg's oldest gallery is a privately run institution spotlighting up-and-coming modern artists.

LISTINGS

Best Places for...

Ⓔ Budget **ⒺⒺ** Midrange **ⒺⒺⒺ** Top End

See p36 for map of locations

Eating

Fast Food

Chingu ⒺⒺ
19 G2
Korean-fusion fast food to sate heavier cravings: fried chicken drenched in spicy sauces, kimchi fries and more. *noon-9.30pm*

Mö-Grill ⒺⒺ
20 F3
Popular venue for the most beloved German fast food, *Currywurst* (sausage with curry ketchup). Locals agree that here the dish is done about the best it's done anywhere. *10am-7pm*

Ramen ⒺⒺ
21 F2
Wood-panelled ramen joint with a small menu, quick service and lots of bar seating – expeditious experience guaranteed. *11.30am-9.30pm*

Seasonal & Local Fare

Ahoi by Steffen Henssler ⒺⒺ
22 F3
German born but always with his eye on the horizon, celebrated local chef Steffen Henssler has made himself a name for sushi making; his menu has fish and chips, salads and burgers too. *10am-6pm*

Daniel Wischer ⒺⒺ
23 C4
A terrific, longstanding place for a quick meal or something more substantial. Grilled fish, a mean fish and chips and outstanding *Fischbrötchen* (fish sandwiches). *11am-9pm Mon-Sat*

Kartoffelkeller ⒺⒺ
24 A6
The country's favourite vegetable becomes a substantial 'food group' here. Potato salad, potato pancakes, potato dumplings – the list goes on. *noon-10pm Thu-Tue*

Nardo's ⒺⒺ
25 C6
Changing share plates mix Mediterranean impulses with German sensibility; expect the likes of scallops in pea soup or German 'antipasti' with sausage and local veggies. *9am-5pm Tue-Sun*

Modern & Fine Dining

Perle ⒺⒺ
26 E5
Venture down a quiet side street for excellent light lunchtime specials. For dinner, one of the best Wiener schnitzels in Hamburg is on offer. *11.30am-3pm & 6-9pm*

Café Paris ⒺⒺⒺ
27 C4
A magnificent 1882 butchers' hall has become an upscale yet relaxed brasserie that's an ideal stop for classical French fare. *9am-11.30pm*

Trific ⒺⒺⒺ
28 B6
Consistently lauded as one of Hamburg's more creative kitchens, Trific

does a small, market-driven menu – maybe corn-fed chicken or regional veal. *noon-3pm & 6-11pm Mon-Fri, 6-11pm Sat*

Drinking

Cafes

Nord Coast Coffee Roasters
 A6

One of Hamburg's growing number of cool, socially conscious coffee roasters, Nord Coast has several locations in the city. Its lovely (and convenient) Deichstrasse outpost is the perfect modern coffee stop. *9am-5pm*

Palang Good Coffee
 F5

At this spot in between Chilehaus' buildings A and B you can stop in for an iced coffee and a bagel after you take in the UNESCO-listed building. *9am-4pm Mon-Fri, from 11am Sat*

Cocktail Bars

Le Lion
 C4

Easily the classiest, most exclusive bar in Hamburg. If there's space, hide out and imbibe – the gin-basil smash is the signature. *6pm-3am Mon-Sat, to 1am Sun*

Bohemian
 A6

Classy Deichstrasse den and terrace specialising in creative (sometimes provocative) concoctions, such as a drink inspired by Charlie Sheen and the rap scene's 'purple drank'. *5pm-1am Mon-Thu, 3pm-2am Fri & Sat, 3pm-midnight Sun*

Shopping

Books & Mementos

Dr Götze Land & Karte
 E2

Browse the world at one of Germany's most renowned map and travel stores. It has an enormous range of English-language books and unique cartographic keepsakes. *10am-7pm Mon-Fri, to 6pm Sat*

Thalia
34 **D3**

One of Hamburg's largest bookshops, this branch of Thalia has a wide selection of English-language books, plus German toys and knickknacks for holiday memories. *10am-8pm Mon-Sat*

Vintage & Rags
35 **G2**

This two-storey vintage clothing store is one of the city's biggest. Thumb through neatly curated brand-name threads plus NFL/MLB jerseys. *11am-8pm Mon-Fri, from 10am Sat*

See p68 for eating, drinking and shopping listings

Explore
Neustadt

Neustadt is one of the best places in Hamburg for shopping and wandering, especially when the sun comes out. Cruise elegant canal-side promenades, then window-shop luxury goods and people-watch in splendid arcades. The Elbemeile section tends to get all the waterside glory, but the Jungfernstieg along the Binnenalster (Inner Alster Lake) is perfect on a blue-sky afternoon – and this is where residents prefer their shoreside scenery, too. Along the Jungfernstieg, little lakeside watering holes are primed for relaxation. Escape the crowds by heading west to explore the region's classical music history or east to Grossneumarkt, a laid-back centre for local life.

Getting Around

Walking
Getting to and around Neustadt is easily accomplished on foot. Combine it with a day in Altstadt (the line between the two is regularly blurred).

Public transport
There's a handful of useful U-Bahn and S-Bahn stations in Neustadt, most conveniently Jungfernstieg. From here connections are possible across the city.

Cycling
Renting a bike and cruising the length of the southern and western shore is a rewarding experience. The views back towards Altstadt (especially at sunset) are magnificent.

★ THE BEST

BAROQUE CHURCH
St Michaelis Kirche (p58)

VENETIAN PROMENADE
Alsterarkaden (p61)

MUSIC MUSEUMS
KomponistenQuartier (p62)

LOCAL MARKET
Grossneumarkt (p67)

JAZZ LAIR
Cotton Club (p66)

Alsterarkaden (p61)
OSCITY/SHUTTERSTOCK

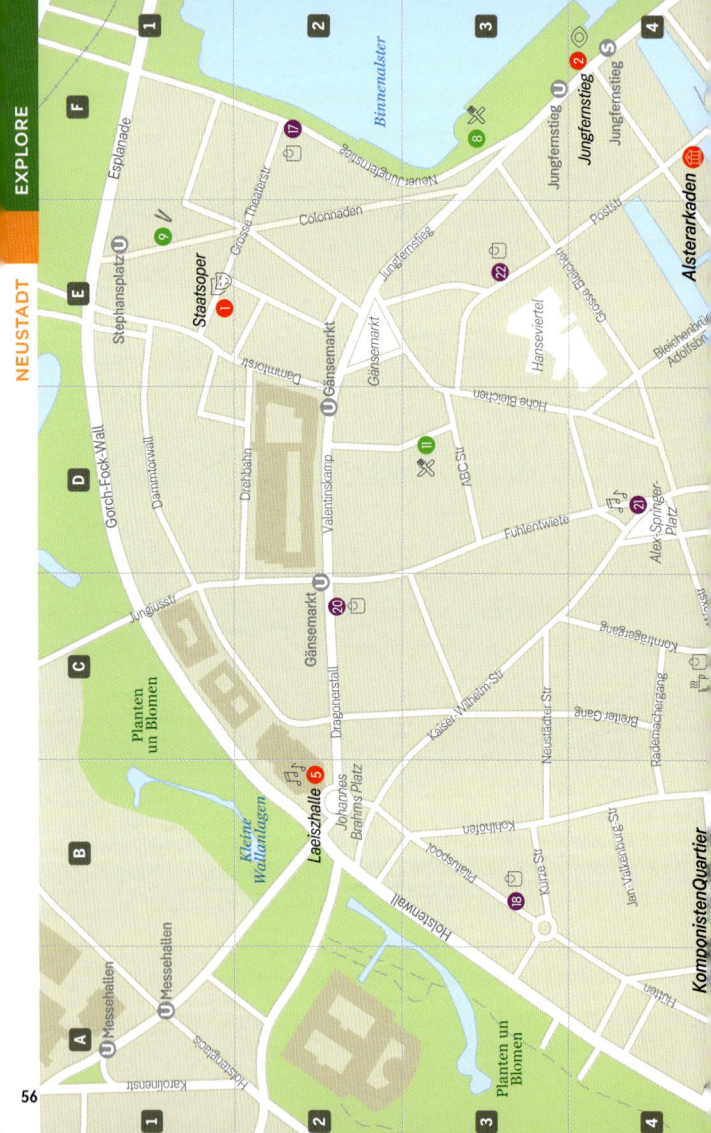

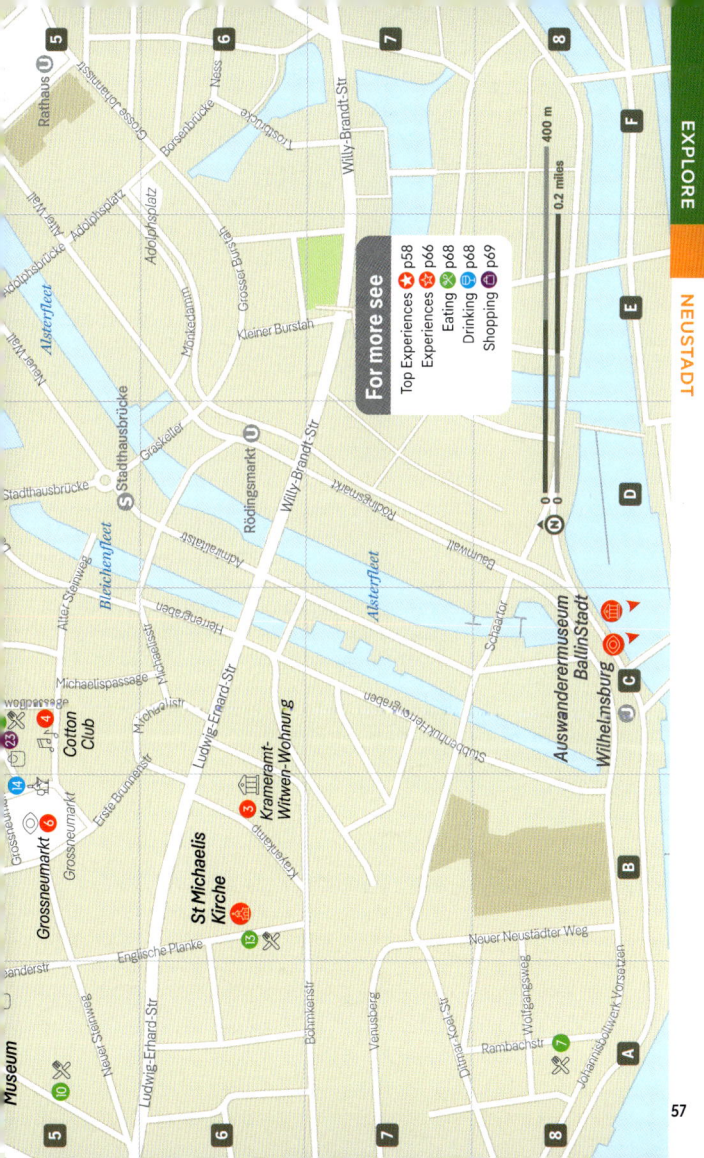

★ TOP EXPERIENCE

St Michaelis Kirche

'**Der Michel**' (The Michael), as it's affectionately known, is one of Hamburg's most recognisable landmarks and northern Germany's largest Protestant Baroque church – it dominates the skyline for miles around. Go up the tower, around the still-functioning nave and inside the crypt; all are worth exploring.

MAP P56 **B6**

PLANNING TIP
The church is in southern Neustadt, close to the port. Enjoy off-the-beaten-track exploration around developing areas and lesser-known sights, like the **Auswanderermuseum BallinStadt** (MAP P56 **C8**; Emigration Museum) and sustainable island district **Wilhelmsburg** (MAP P56 **C8**).

Architecture & History

St Michaelis Kirche is the third church to be built on this site. What you see today is an early-20th-century replica of the two previous versions, which were destroyed by fire. Composer Johannes Brahms was baptised on 26 May 1833 in the previous version. The steeple stands 132m high and has historically been used for orientation by ships sailing down the Elbe River. The clock is the largest such timepiece in Germany; its dominating face also once helped ships navigate along the Elbe River.

Tower

Energetic visitors will want to climb to the viewing platform 83m above street level, but there's also a lift that will take you up in no time. The views are simply wonderful, and it's worth spending as long as you can up here to pick out Hamburg's canals, waterways and other landmarks. The views towards the harbour are particularly memorable, especially with the Elbphilharmonie (p89) in all its glory.

FOOTAGECLIPS/SHUTTERSTOCK

Sanctuary

There are prettier church interiors in Germany and, truth be told, St Michaelis' main sanctuary is cavernous and quite unadorned, as is the Protestant way. But what stands out about the inside is its sheer scale. Adopting the classic cathedral layout of a Latin cross plan, the space has room for 2500 seats. There are also an astonishing five organs. Despite the general austerity of style, the Baroque altar and pulpit, the elaborate pulpit staircase and the marble baptismal font are worth close examination; the altar is 20m high and depicts scenes from Christ's life.

QUICK BREAK
Opposite the entrance to St Michaelis Kirche, and in business since 1795, the **Old Commercial Room** (p68) is where you'll find Hamburg's best *Labskaus* (a meat, fish and potato stew).

TALJAT DAVID/SHUTTERSTOCK

CONCERTS

The church's diverse and experiential concert programme is worth exploring whether you're observant or not. Daily midday worship is always accompanied by the monster organs. On Sunday, in a centuries-old ceremony, a traditional chorale rings up from the tower. Finally, the crypt is the perfect, atmospheric setting for compositions by Bach, Beethoven and of course Brahms, who was baptised at St Michaelis.

Crypt

Even though it costs extra, don't forgo the rather crowded crypt, where nearly 2500 luminaries are buried, including composer Carl Philipp Emanuel Bach (son of the more famous Johann). Restored at the turn of the century, the crypt (pictured above) was used as an air-raid shelter during WWII. These days it hosts church services (the dwindling congregation gets rather lost upstairs) and concerts, and has an engaging multimedia exhibit on the city's history.

Scan this QR code for the musical schedule.

⭐ TOP EXPERIENCE

Alsterarkaden

Not to be missed in Neustadt is the sophisticated **Alsterarkaden** along the waterfront. The Venetian-inspired shopping arcade's archways reflect off the Alsterfleet canal – a mesmering sight, especially when the swans dip and dive about. Boutiques and restaurants are tucked between the arcade's arches.

MAP P56 **F4**

Shopping & Swans

The highlight of Neustadt's busy shopping area, the pillared Alsterarkaden shelters upscale shops and cafes along the Alsterfleet canal to the **Jungfernstieg** (p66). It's home to Hamburg's lunching crowds, luxury shoppers and sightseeing visitors. They're not the only ones showing off: white and black swans can be found preening and paddling along the water. In medieval times it was said that if swans could be seen on the Alster, Hamburg would maintain its freedom and sovereignty.

Art Nouveau Arcade

Adjacent to the Alsterarkaden is the **Mellin Passage**, Hamburg's oldest shopping arcade, which connects to the upscale **Neuer Wall** shopping street. This passage is worth a peek for its ornate 19th-century Art Nouveau ceiling frescoes and stained-glass windows (unexpectedly discovered during restoration following a fire).

Around & Away

The Alsterfleet, connecting the Inner Alster and the Elbe River, is the historic boundary between Altstadt and Neustadt. Follow the Jungfernstieg northwest for waterfront greenery and residential vibes or go the opposite way, along Ballindamm, to **Hamburger Kunsthalle** (p43) and Hamburg Hauptbahnhof (about 1km).

PLANNING TIP

The Alsterfleet canal separates Altstadt and Neustadt. From the Rathaus (p38), you can easily reach the Alsterarkaden via the overwater walkway left of the front public square.

Scan this QR code for a self-guided walking tour linking Neustadt to Alstadt.

★ TOP EXPERIENCE

KomponistenQuartier

A string of museums in restored 18th-century townhouses along Peterstrasse make up the **KomponistenQuartier** *(Composers' Quarter; adult/child €11/2)*, a unique ensemble celebrating Hamburg's orchestral heritage. Displaying artefacts, instruments and more, each museum focuses on the life and work of a composer who left their mark on the city. KomponistenQuartier museums are closed on Mondays.

MAP P56 **A4**

PLANNING TIP
Wander out of the Komponisten-Quartier and you'll find several **music stores** (p69) in the surrounding area selling everything from handmade instruments to sheet music.

Scan this QR code for the KomponistenQuartier website.

Music Museums

The most famous among the six townhouse exhibitions is dedicated to **Johannes Brahms** *(Peterstrasse 39),* who was born and raised in Hamburg. Founded in 1971, the Komponisten-Quartier's other museums on **Georg Philipp Telemann and Carl Philipp Emanuel Bach** *(Peterstrasse 31),* **Johann Adolf Hasse, Fanny and Felix Mendelssohn, and Gustav Mahler** *(Peterstrasse 29)* have developed over more recent years.

All made a significant musical contribution to Hamburg, composing everything from operas to church music, across a range of classical styles. The museums' collections go beyond traditional displays to feature historical instruments and also personal belongings such as manuscripts and letters revealing the composers' creative processes. The Composers' Quarter is a reminder that the Elbphilharmonie (p89) is just one of many notes that make up Hamburg's resounding orchestral heritage.

BILDAGENTUR-ONLINE/ALAMY

Brahms Museum

The **Brahms Museum** (MAP P56 **A5**; pictured above), once standing alone but integrated into the KomponistenQuartier in 2015, is considered the quarter's most significant exhibition. Globally renowned Johannes Brahms (1833–1897), considered one of the 'three Bs' of German music along with Beethoven and Bach, was born in Hamburg and maintained lifelong ties with the city.

While the house where he was born was destroyed in 1943, the 18th-century building at Peterstrasse 39 makes for a fitting tribute. All manner of original Brahms memorabilia is on display, including a table piano from the 1860s on which he gave lessons to students.

QUICK BREAK

Head east to the **Grossneumarkt** (p67), where you'll find stalls on Wednesday and Saturday mornings, plus **Thämer's** (p65), an unpretentious German restaurant with lots of outside seating.

Notably Neustadt

Canal-side window-shopping is only a small part of Neustadt. For a real glimpse into the lives of neighbourhood residents, head west around Wextrasse. Here you'll find local life set to a quiet, steady pace. Hamburg's history and traditions – and most notably, its classical music heritage – are harmoniously woven through.

START	END	LENGTH
KomponistenQuartier	Hummerstand im Hanseviertel	1km; 30 minutes

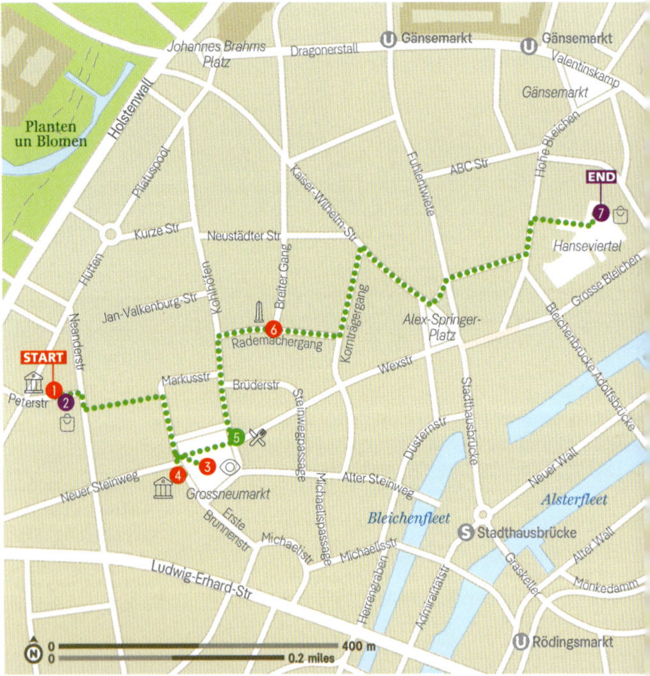

1 Classical Museums
Start your stroll around Neustadt in its most fascinating historic area. Around the **KomponistenQuartier** (Composers' Quarter; p62), 18th-century merchant houses now play home to museums dedicated to Brahms, Bach, Mendelssohn and more.

2 Artisan Studio
Still in the KomponistenQuartier, take a peek into the **studio** (p69) of master violin-maker Pia-Maria von Ketelhodt, opened in 2024. Inside you'll find the Hamburg-born craftswoman woodworking and carving instruments with precision.

3 Market Square
The leafy **Grossneumarkt** (p67) is a relaxed change from the more chichi canal-side parts of Neustadt. It comes to life with market stalls and eclectic food trucks on Wednesday and Saturday.

4 Historic Pharmacy
The still-functioning **Pelikan Apotheke** (one of Germany's oldest pharmacies) has been around since 1656. Wander in to admire splendid period touches, such as high ceilings and rich wood panelling, framing today's daily business.

5 Cake Stop
Sit down for cake or German *Flammkuchen* (flatbread) at **Thämer's**. The restaurant occupies a prime spot with dozens of covered tables on the square; in the evening, it becomes a classic *Kneipe* (traditional dive bar; p68). There's an extensive beer and wine selection, and the kitchen specialises in hearty German cuisine.

6 Memorial Fountain
Take in the **Hummel Memorial**, dedicated to local resident Hans Hummel, who worked as a water carrier in Neustadt in the 19th and early 20th centuries (before a pipe system existed). He would tell mischievous kids to 'kiss his behind' – and his memorial depicts him hoisting a yoke and water buckets while a child moons him. Once one of many 'Hummel' statues, this Hans is now a rare find. In 2006 several sculptures were auctioned, with proceeds going to support Hamburg's homeless people.

7 Seafood Heaven
In the Hanseviertel shopping arcade, relax on a barstool at seafood stand **Hummerstand im Hanseviertel**. For over 50 years it's been a local favourite for grilled lobster, oysters, mussels and other prepared seafood dishes washed down with glasses of *sekt* (sparkling wine) or Champagne. On the first Thursday of the month the arcade hosts a dance evening with music and seafood bites.

EXPERIENCES

Indulge in Ballet & Opera at the Staatsoper
OPERA HOUSE

MAP: ❶ P56 **E1**

Among the world's most respected opera houses, **Hamburg's Staatsoper** *(staatsoper-hamburg.de; box office 10am-6pm Mon-Sat, plus 90min prior to performances; tickets from €4)* has been directed by the likes of Gustav Mahler and Karl Böhm during its 325-year-plus history. The grand modernist music theatre is the home of the Hamburg Philharmonic State Orchestra and the Hamburg Ballet. Its massive main auditorium, with capacity for 1690 guests, ensures tickets are usually easy to come by. Seating is priced by category; the cheapest can go for as little as €4, while the best cost up to €258.

Walk along the Jungfernstieg
LAKESIDE PROMENADE

MAP: ❷ P56 **F4**

Neustadt, seamlessly blending with Altstadt in the posh surrounds of the Binnenalster, is at its best along the **Jungfernstieg promenade**. Leading up and around to the southern side of Hamburg Hauptbahnhof (on its northern side you'll find Altstadt), it's the perfect spot to stretch your legs before jumping on a train. Even better, it's an alternative route to head back to the station if you've already strolled along St Georg's Lange Reihe (p78).

Enjoy the leafy, shaded pathway; there are plentiful spots to picnic or sit along the water, too. The outdoor tables of the cafes and bars close to the waterfront, though appealing, tend to be overpriced and touristy. The pavilion dining at Alex (p68) is an exception.

Visit Historic Almshouses
HIDDEN ALLEYWAY

In an alley off Krayenkamp 10 is a row of tiny half-timbered houses from the 17th century. For nearly 200 years these were almshouses for the widows of members of the Guild of Small Shopkeepers. Today they house shops and restaurants, plus a little historical museum, the **Krameramt-Witwen-Wohnung** (MAP: ❸ P56 **B6**; *shmh.de; adult/child €4/free*) that's open Wednesday to Sunday.

Take in Live Jazz at Cotton Club
JAZZ CLUB

MAP: ❹ P56 **C5**

It has moved around a lot in its time, but wherever **Cotton Club** *(cotton-club.de; ticket prices vary)* has been in Hamburg, it has been reliable for live jazz in all its forms – with some blues, swing, Dixieland and other genres thrown in. In music-centric Neustadt, the city's oldest jazz club has truly found the perfect home. Buy tickets online *(tixforgigs.com)* or at the door. Gigs start at 8pm.

Attend a Performance at the Laeiszhalle
CONCERT HALL

MAP: 5 P56 B2

Built in 1908, the **Laeiszhalle** (elbphilharmonie.de/de/laeiszhalle; ticket prices vary) was Hamburg's premier address for classical concerts and opera for decades. That mantle has passed to the extraordinary new Elbphilharmonie (p89), but this splendid neo-Baroque edifice still hosts a regular calendar of classical performances.

The Elbphilharmonie and Laeiszhalle are under joint directorship, and though the former gets more glory, Laeiszhalle has a historic charm that sets it apart. Unlike much of the city, the structure survived the bombing of Hamburg; occupying British forces used the building as studios for a military broadcasting station and stored over 60,000 jazz records in the Brahms-Foyer.

Dine & Snack at Grossneumarkt
LOCAL MARKET

MAP: 6 P56 B5

Once the hub of Neustadt, the large, leafy **Grossneumarkt** is pretty quiet these days, although market stalls on Wednesday and Saturday mornings liven things up. (The market food trucks alone are worth a trip to enjoy international fare from Thai curry to quesadillas, African food and Polish *pierogi*).

Established between 1624 and 1660 during the expansion of Hamburg's city fortifications, the Grossneumarkt was one of four central squares in what was once the still-developing Neustadt. Initially the square was primarily used for military activities such as *Soldatenhandel* (soldier trade), a practice where German states leased soldiers to wealthier nations.

Over time the Grossneumarkt evolved into a lively market square. One of its most frequent vendors is said to have been the 19th-century German animal trader Carl Hagenbeck (1844–1913), acclaimed for developing modern zoo designs comprising open enclosures without bars. The story goes he sold exotic animals here.

NOT SO NEW ANY MORE

The name 'Neustadt' (New City) is something of a misnomer – though it wasn't always. Developed in the early 17th century, the district was an expansion beyond Hamburg's medieval city walls to accommodate growing trade and population. The Binnenalster (Inner Alster Lake) waterfront is such a fixture of Hamburg's Neustadt that many locals don't know the origin of the name of its promenade, the Jungfernstieg. It was so called because in ancient times families used to bring their unmarried daughters *(jungfern)* to the promenade for a stroll.

LISTINGS

Best Places for...

€ Budget €€ Midrange €€€ Top End

See p56 for map of locations

Eating

International Dining

Lusitano €€
7 A8

Little restaurant in Hamburg's old Portuguese neighbourhood capturing the bright flavours of the Mediterranean. Dishes such as spicy sausages and pasta are well executed, but the seafood is the real star. Book ahead. *noon-10pm Mon & Wed-Sat*

Alex €€€
8 F3

While the breakfast buffets at this German restaurant chain are satisfying, the location is the reason you'll go. It occupies the 1799 Alsterpavillon, a lakeside historic gem – its original cafe is credited with introducing ice cream to Germany. *8am-1am Mon-Thu, to 2am Fri & Sat, from 9am Sun*

Matsumi €€€
9 E1

Celebrated sushi chef Hideaki Morita creates excellent Japanese fare at this 2nd-floor restaurant. There are also various teriyaki grills and a sake menu worth exploring. *noon-1.30pm & 6-9.30 pm Tue-Sat*

Petit Bonheur €€€
10 A5

A French wine bistro for romantic affairs – *coq au vin* is a crowd favourite. Beautiful red-walled interiors and white tablecloths; antique furnishings abound. *noon-11pm Mon-Fri, from 5pm Sat*

Casse Croute €€€
11 D3

Elegant, romantically lit restaurant for north German cuisine served with French culinary flair. A long wine list and the best *moules frites* in Hamburg. *noon-10pm Tue-Thu, noon-9pm Mon & Fri, 5-10pm Sat*

German Fare

Zum Spätzle €
12 C5

Specialising in *Spätzle* (a pasta-like dish from Swabia) and *Maultaschen* (a filled pasta, also from further south), this is a terrific place to sample German regional cuisine. Small dining room. *noon-10pm*

Old Commercial Room €€
13 B6

Around since 1795, this fine bastion of tradition has long been serving some of Hamburg's best *Labskaus* (meat, fish and potato stew). Yes, it's touristy, but the food is excellent. It's opposite St Michaelis Kirche. *noon-11pm Mon-Sat, to 10pm Sun*

Drinking

Cafes & Bars

Herr Buhbe
14 B5

One of the oldest wine cellars in the city and

the sister bar to upstairs Thämer's (p65), Herr Buhbe is always a solid choice. Plentiful draught beer, a decent wine list of predominantly French and German options, and a good selection of mid-shelf spirits. *noon-3pm & 6pm-midnight Mon-Sat*

Public Coffee Roasters
 C4

Lovers of fine coffee consider it worth crossing town to this cafe for the quiet, casual atmosphere and the selection of great coffees straight from the roastery. *8.30am-6pm Mon-Fri, 10am-5.30pm Sat & Sun*

Shopping

Speciality Boutiques

Anne Zimmer
(16) C4

This gorgeous little boutique selling handmade gold and other jewellery is a lovely counterpoint to the luxury international brands that dominate Neustadt. Beautiful homewares are also found in the light, airy space. *11am-7pm Tue-Fri, to 4pm Sat*

Apropos the Concept Store
(17) F2

Perfectly at home next to the palatial Fairmont Vier Jahreszeiten Hamburg hotel, this luxury concept store assembles a fine, well-curated portfolio of pieces from top luxury brands under one roof. *11am-7pm Mon-Sat*

Music Stores

Geigenbau Matthias Tödtmann
(18) B3

String instrument specialist Tödtmann crafts and repairs violins, violas, cellos and bows in his evocative workshop. Restorations are also a focal point. *noon-6pm Tue-Fri*

Geigenbau von Ketelhodt
(19) A5

This studio is helmed by Hamburg-born master violin maker Pia-Maria von Ketelhodt. It's located right on Peterstrasse in the KomponistenQuartier (p62). *by appointment Wed-Fri*

Geigenbau Winterling
(20) C2

An essential part of the city's musical fabric since 1890, this workshop houses exquisite stringed instruments, including some extraordinary historic pieces that have been restored here. Note that prices are steep; this is not a place for casual visitors. *2-6.30pm Thu, from 10am Fri*

Tutti Fagotti
(21) D4

Europe's largest on-site collection of bassoons and contrabassoons plus every bassoon-related accessory under the sun. Also provides full servicing and repair. *9am-3pm Mon-Fri*

Gourmet Treats

Mutterland
(22) E3

'Made in Germany' gourmet delicatessen selling tempting, beautifully packaged foods (jams, chocolates) and liquors. Pick up the Monkey 47 Black Forest gin. *8am-7pm Mon-Fri, from 10am Sat*

Tobias Strauch Weinkontor
(23) C5

Hamburg culinary celebrity Tobias Strauch knows what he's talking about when it comes to wine. His carefully chosen selection of mostly European bottles is one of the best you'll find. *11am-7pm Tue-Fri, from 10am Sat*

See p81 for eating, drinking and shopping listings

Explore
St Georg

With all its character and contradictions, St Georg is Hamburg in microcosm. The restaurants and bars of lively main thoroughfare Lange Reihe are popular with LGBTIQ+ locals, and the area has grown increasingly multicultural in recent years. Around lunchtime, St Georg offers an appealingly relaxed atmosphere, but the mood shifts from early afternoon. Lange Reihe's daytime boutiques and cafes start slowing down, passing the baton to venues such as gay institution Café Gnosa, which ramp up the energy. Soon enough, the cocktail bars are buzzing. On Friday, the neighbourhood market is a local highlight.

Getting Around

 Walking

Just about everywhere in St Georg is within easy walking distance of the Hauptbahnhof; hotels and hostels are mostly clustered at the station (southwestern) end of the neighbourhood.

 Train

St Georg lies behind the Hauptbahnhof. Lange Reihe makes for a perfect bite and stroll before or after catching a train.

 Cycling

Scoring some wheels is the perfect way to explore off the Lange Reihe – there are some fabulous secrets to discover. StadtRad rents bikes at the Hauptbahnhof.

Hansaplatz (p80)
DAVID TALJAT/ALAMY

THE BEST

ART MUSEUM
Museum für Kunst und Gewerbe (p74)

SHOPPING STREET
Lange Reihe (p78)

ARTISAN ARCADE
Koppel 66 (p79)

BAKERY
Café Gnosa (p79)

REGIONAL LUNCH
Fräulein Fritz (p81)

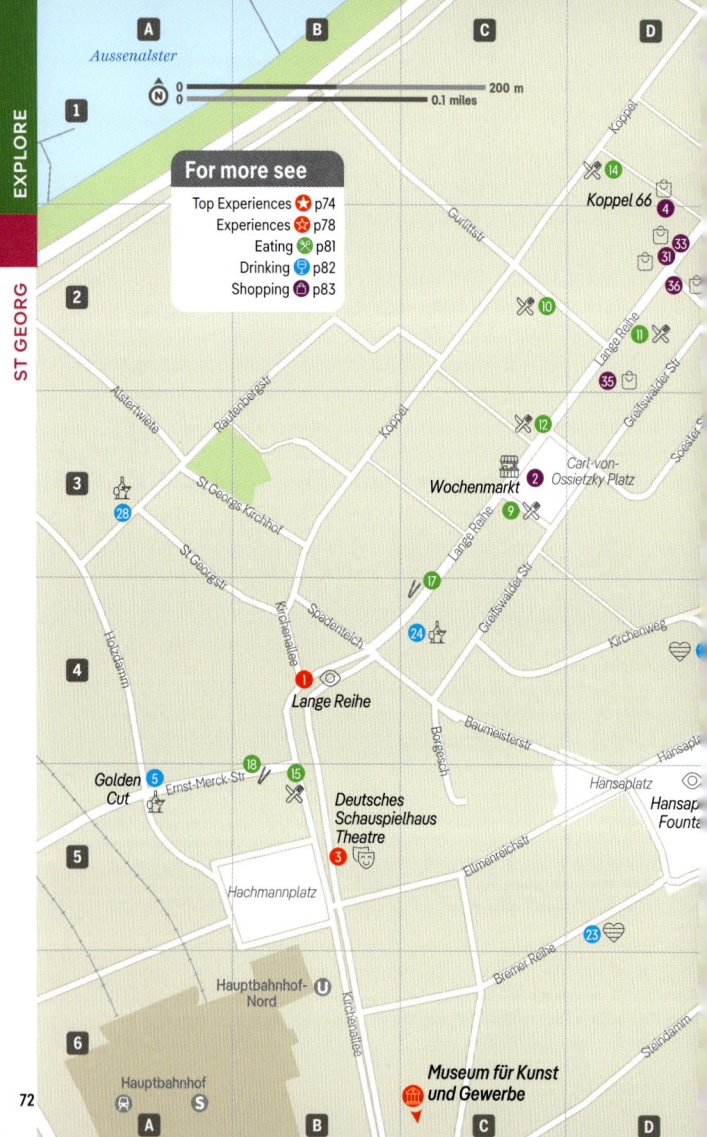

St Marien-Dom

ST GEORG

★ TOP EXPERIENCE

Museum für Kunst und Gewerbe

The **Museum for Art & Industry** *(mkg-hamburg.de; adult/child €14/free)* is St Georg's main attraction – and it's a gem. Here you can marvel at some 600,000 gorgeous, delicate handicrafts of all shapes and sizes, sourced from 4000 years of human history around the world.

MAP P72 **C6**

Collection & History

Known as the MK&G for short, the museum is a creative paradise. Running from the medieval period to the pop art movement, the vast collection includes artisan-made sculpture, furniture, fashion, jewellery, posters, porcelain, musical instruments and household objects. Highlights include ancient Greco-Roman and Italian ceramics, 14th-century Islamic art from a mausoleum in modern-day Uzbekistan and a *chashitsu* (traditional Japanese tea room) that was the first of its kind to be shown in a European museum.

The MK&G was established in 1887. Its first director, Justus Brinckmann, aimed to create a place that would inspire local artisans and industry. Acquiring objects from international exhibitions, world's fairs, auctions and art dealers has curated an eclectic mix proudly shaped by a broad array of societal influences.

Jugendstil

Jugendstil (German Art Nouveau) emerged as an 'aesthetic antidote' to impersonal Industrial Revolution–era mass production. The term came from the magazine *Die Jugend* (Youth), which showcased how objects could be beautiful and functional. The MK&G houses the most comprehensive *Jugendstil* collection in northern Germany.

PLANNING TIP
The museum is one of five Hamburg art institutions included in the **Art Mile pass** *(kunstmeile-hamburg.de; 3-day ticket €35)*. It's a great deal even if you're only planning to visit a couple of museums.

Scan this QR code to view the temporary exhibitions.

SCHOENING/ALAMY

Highlights include *Swan Carpet* (1897) by Otto Eckmann and the Paris Room, a salon decorated with *Jugendstil* pieces sourced from the 1900 Paris world's fair. The room is the perfect example of the *Jugendstil* principle of *Gesamtkunstwerk* (total work of art).

The Modern (1914–1945)

The MK&G's German Modernism section comprises art movements that emerged in the historical contexts of WWI, the Weimar Republic, the rise of the Third Reich and WWII.

Expressionist works such as the abstract animal sculptures of Richard Haizmann (declared by the Nazis to be a 'degenerate artist') and everyday objects of the minimalistic Bauhaus style (similarly, the Nazis denounced the movement as politically dangerous) endure as important examples of German resistance through design.

QUICK BREAK
Walk through leafy Carl-Legien-Platz park to **Fräulein Fritz** (p81), a beautiful whitewashed lunch restaurant specialising in modern German fare that breaks the mould. Meals are delightfully light and nourishing.

WALKING TOUR

St Georg: Alternative & Arty

St Georg is a window on inner-urban Hamburg. At once newly multicultural and the heart of the city's gay scene, it's sometimes gritty, sometimes offbeat. Its centrepiece is Lange Reihe, and lots of what's good about St Georg happens along and close to this street. Eclectic and lively, the neighbourhood exudes a real sense of community.

START	END	LENGTH
Heilige Dreieinigkeitskirche	Kyti Voo	450m; 30 minutes

1 Baroque Church

St Georg's **Heilige Dreieinigkeitskirche** is a small Baroque treasure. The medieval site of worship (rebuilt after WWII air raids – the tower is its only original feature) is beloved for its wonderful acoustics and busy concert schedule. The gigantic, rainbow-painted letters spelling *Liebe* (love) at its entrance make a popular photo op.

2 Chic Cafe

St Georg is at its most modern at **Mutterland Stammhaus** (p81), a stylish daytime venue with sit-down brunch, a delicatessen and an upstairs cafe. Grabbing coffee here is a quick stop, but expect a queue if you'd like to have a meal. The 'Made in Germany' shop has beautifully packaged gourmet treats (jams, chocolates) and drinks (try the Monkey 47 gin, distilled in the Black Forest).

3 Square with Fountain

Shabby-chic **Hansaplatz** (p80) is the neighbourhood's hub. True to the area's roots, the square's elegant central **fountain** attracts locals from all walks of life. Completed in 1878, the landmark depicts important figures in Hamburg's past, including Emperors Constantine the Great and Charlemagne, and is surmounted by a figure showing the might of the medieval Hanseatic League.

4 Eat Street

Follow the **Lange Reihe** (p78), St Georg's main vein, and let the sidewalk terraces tempt you to stop and take a break. Look no further than here to find one of Hamburg's gastronomic hot spots: choose among cool cafes and eclectic cuisines from Italian to Thai.

5 Organic Market

The weekly sustainable **Wochenmarkt** (p78) on Carl-von-Ossietzky Platz, adds a burst of life to Friday afternoons. In the heart of St Georg, the market is mostly a neighbourhood residents' affair for shopping organic farm produce. The vibrant atmosphere is a draw in its own right.

6 Artisan Shops

Arguably Hamburg's premier collection of art-and-craft stores, the arcade at **Koppel 66** (p79) is worth forging past Lange Reihe's buzzy gastronomy (at least for a little while). An elegant, old-world haven for modern ateliers and designers' boutiques, it has intriguing options from hat-makers to artisan jewellery and handmade cosmetics.

7 Premier Cocktail Bar

One of the city's best cocktail bars, **Kyti Voo** (p83) attracts a mixed crowd with its generous happy hour, which runs from 5pm to 8pm, and weekend hours until at least 2am.

EXPERIENCES

Stroll the Lange Reihe — SHOPPING STREET

MAP: ① P72 **B4**

You'll want to spend most of your time in St Georg wandering the **Lange Reihe** thoroughfare, where the pulse of local life is what it's all about.

Restaurants, bars, cafes and shopping boutiques abound. Choosing one will be your toughest task, but pavement terraces – and eyeing the food and drink of other diners – will help you make an educated decision. Another tip: stroll the entire street before choosing a spot.

Outdoor tables always come with a side of free entertainment: front-row people-watching of St Georg's diverse *Menschenauflauf* (literally, 'a crowd of people stew').

Visit a Sustainable Market — FRESH PRODUCE

Weekly eco-market the **Wochenmarkt** (MAP: ② P72 C3; *food-lovers-market.de; 2-6.30pm Fri*) enlivens Friday afternoons in the heart of St Georg. Local vendors set up stands for organic produce, handmade crafts, natural cosmetics and other sustainable wares. Slurping up oysters and organic and biodynamic wines is a delight.

Occasional sustainability workshops (usually in German) are held on composting, upcycling and the like. Sometimes the market shifts to Friday morning – check the website.

Attend Germany's Largest Theatre — THEATRE COMPANY

Germany's largest theatre, **Deutsches Schauspielhaus Theatre** (MAP: ③ P72 **B5**; *schauspielhaus.de; tickets from €20*) presents imaginative interpretations of classic plays (by Shakespeare, Goethe, Chekhov et al) alongside new works. It's one of the city's most dynamic cultural spaces.

 ST GEORG'S HISTORY

St Georg is one of Hamburg's oldest neighbourhoods. In the 12th century the district developed around the St Georg Hospital, where sufferers of Hansen's disease (leprosy) received treatment. The hospital was located outside the medieval city walls to contain the spread of the illness. Following 19th-century industrialisation and urban expansion, St Georg was integrated into Hamburg proper. In the late 20th century it became an artists' and migrants' hub thanks to affordable housing and the revitalisation of commercial space. Today St Georg is Hamburg's most multicultural neighbourhood. City statistics from 2022 indicate that 100 nationalities are represented here.

A CITY OF MIGRANTS

As a port city, Hamburg has always prided itself on being worldly and open to new faces. Yet 2015's unprecedented influx of millions of immigrants to Germany presented challenges, with impacts on public housing, welfare and integration in general. In 2016 Hamburg accepted 40,000 refugees – more than the British government committed to allow into the entire UK over a five-year period. Many immigrants come from Muslim countries; Turkey and Afghanistan are the largest and third-largest source countries respectively. Poland comes in second. By one estimate, one-third of Hamburg's population is now foreign born.

Shop in an Artisan Arcade   BEAUTIFUL BOUTIQUES

MAP: 4 P72 D2

Former machine factory **Koppel 66** (MAP: 4 P72 **D2**; *koppel66.de*) is the city's finest gathering of arts-and-crafts boutiques and ateliers. Various workshops maintain the brick walls, exposed beams and other charming elements of the building's past life.

Studio Maals specialises in functional tableware handmade from clay and porcelain; it also offers pottery workshops. At **Gaschler Hat Design**, choose among fedoras made of Panamanian straw and fanciful 1920s-inspired cloches. The handmade, olive oil-based soaps at **Zoe Seifen** make great souvenirs.

Dance at Golden Cut   NIGHTCLUB

MAP: 5 P72 **A5**

One of Hamburg's top clubs, **Golden Cut** (*golden-cut.club*) has a strict door policy and lines can be long. Some of the best local and touring DJs turn up here. Expect house, R&B and hip-hop and the odd big-show afterparty.

Savour Cake & LGBTIQ+ History at Café Gnosa   BRUNCH & AFTERNOON TEA

MAP: 6 P72 **E1**

With its abstract art and in-house bakery, **Café Gnosa** (*@cafe_gnosa*) draws an affable mixed crowd. Breakfast is served until 4pm, and the cafe is also the perfect place to indulge in the German afternoon tradition of *Kaffee und Kuchen* (coffee and cake) – the on-site bakery conjures up a daily-changing selection of delectable cakes and pastries. Try for an outside table.

Established around 1900, the cafe is named after the Gnosa family who took it over in 1939. In the 1970s the space became known as a gay-friendly venue – progressive for the time. By the 1980s Gnosa had become widely recognised as one of the city's first openly gay cafes. LGBTIQ+ events hosted here include the first solo show of legendary German photographer Wolfgang Tillmans in 1988.

People-watch at Hansaplatz
PUBLIC SQUARE

MAP: 7 P72 **D5**

Though Lange Reihe gets all the fame, the neighbourhood's beating heart is most authentically **Hansaplatz**. Long a rendezvous spot, the public square draws an *Eintopf* (one-pot stew) of local life across park benches and greenery.

In 2011 major renovations made the square much more attractive and enjoyable – although locals might say the makeover was a harbinger of St Georg's gentrification struggle.

Visit St Maria's Crypt
BISHOPS' RESTING PLACE

Constructed between 1890 and 1893 in neo-Romanesque, medievally inspired style, **St Marien-Dom** (MAP: 8 P72 **F2**; *mariendom hamburg.de; free*) was the first Catholic church to be built in Hamburg after the Reformation. Inside the three-aisled basilica, blindingly white walls reach to the heavens, punctuated by dramatic rounded arches and stone columns.

Marvel at the grand neo-Baroque organ above the entrance and, at the front of the cathedral, take in the altar framed by its golden arches up close. To the right is a modern extension added in 2012. Down the hallway, a door leads to a crypt and columbarium beneath the altar. Several bishops of Hamburg have been laid to rest here in bronze-covered urns. The sprawling space, with exposed brick walls, a pebble-stone floor and minimal lighting, can accommodate up to 1500 urns.

Look closely at the crypt's centrepiece, an agate altar slab: embedded in it is a 170-million-year-old fish fossil symbolising the early Christian *Ichthys* (fish) sign.

 GENTRIFICATION IN ST GEORG

Once made up of large 19th-century apartment blocks for Hamburg's upper-middle classes, St Georg hit a nadir in the 1970s. Thoughtless postwar reconstruction combined with increased crime to give the area a seedy reputation. In later years St Georg emerged as a working-class, socially diverse neighbourhood. New arrivals from Turkey, the Middle East, Africa and beyond shaped the area with small businesses at the same time as it became Hamburg's de facto LGBTIQ+ heartland. Diversity remains a defining feature of St Georg, but gentrification now imperils its cultural landscape. Soaring rents have displaced vulnerable communities, threatening the area's multicultural and queer identity.

LISTINGS

Best Places for...

❶ Budget ❷❷ Midrange ❸❸❸ Top End

Eating

On Lange Reihe

Otto's Burger ❶
9 C3

Beef, chicken and veggie burgers with special mayos and decadent fixings are on offer at Otto's. Craft beer too. *noon-10pm Mon-Thu, to 10.30pm Fri & Sat, to 9.30pm Sun*

Cafe Gitane ❷❷
10 C2

Tasteful retro furnishings deck out this appealing cafe-wine bar. Its seasonal menu ranges from the Mediterranean to the North Sea. *5-11pm Mon-Sat*

Cox ❸❸❸
11 D2

Behind its opaque glass doors, this upmarket bistro with fluted columns and period decor was part of St Georg's gentrification vanguard. Its changing menu of dishes reflects seasonal foods and influences from across the continent. *noon-2.30pm & 6.30-10.30pm Mon-Fri, 6.30-10.30pm Sat & Sun*

Das Dorf ❸❸❸
12 C3

Traditional, wood-panelled Das Dorf serves delicious northern German specialities such as *Labskaus*. *6-11pm Tue-Fri, from 5pm Sat & Sun*

Off Lange Reihe

Fräulein Fritz ❷❷
13 H5

It's well worth venturing off the Lange Reihe for Fritz' changing lunch menu, fast service and high-quality regional produce. *11.30am-3pm Mon-Fri*

Café Koppel ❷❷
14 D1

With a summer garden, vegetarian Café Koppel is a refined oasis. The menu could be an ad for the fertile fields of northern Germany, as all dishes are made with fresh seasonal ingredients. *10am-11pm*

Mutterland Stammhaus ❷❷
15 B5

Inviting relaxed brunches on leather chairs, this industrial-chic space with a nod to Art Deco is St Georg's most modern eatery. The upstairs cafe has a quieter ambience. *7am-8pm Mon-Sat, 9am-6pm Sun*

International Dining

Casa di Roma ❷❷
16 E1

One of the classier Italian restaurants among many in St Georg, Casa di Roma delivers cool, contemporary digs and well-priced pasta dishes. Meat or fish mains are much pricier but well worth it; the menu changes regularly. *11.30am-midnight*

Yume Ramen ❷❷
17 C4

Cosy Yume serves up heaping bowls of Japanese- and Korean-inspired ramen dishes. It's a popular choice for vegetarians and vegans. *noon-10.30pm*

Restaurant Herr He €€
 B5

Modern Chinese restaurant Herr He is beloved for dim sum and Cantonese-style dishes. Go for the shrimp rice noodle rolls and pork belly. *noon-10.30pm*

Injera €€
 G3

As the name suggests, *injera* (a spongy flatbread) is the house speciality at this authentic Eritrean and Ethiopian place. Enjoy it with flavourful stews and slow-cooked vegetables. *noon-10pm Sun-Thu, to 11pm Fri & Sat*

L'Amira €€
 F5

Family-owned L'Amira serves Syrian and Lebanese cuisine: falafel, hummus, kebabs and other Middle Eastern flavours. The dining room is large and buzzy. *8am-midnight Sun-Thu, to 1am Fri & Sat*

Singh €€
 E5

Curries, biryanis and tandoori are the top choices at Singh, which serves a wide variety of traditional Indian dishes. It's a local favourite for its generous portions; the flamboyant decor may divide opinion. *4-11pm Sun-Fri, from noon Sat*

Chopan €€
 E6

Casual Chopan offers Turkish and Middle Eastern food cooked with love. Go for *döner* kebabs, *lahmacun* (akin to Turkish pizza) or a make-your-own *meze* platter. *noon-11pm*

Drinking

Gay Bars

Bar Kunterbunt
 D5

If you're not ready to go home, Kunterbunt's got you covered. The dive bar's name ('colourful' in German) has regulars who are *very* much that. *10am-midnight Tue, 24hr Wed-Sun*

M&V Bar
 C4

The drinks menu is like a designer catalogue at this grand old St Georg bar that has been beautifully restored. Settle into one of the wooden booths, smell the freesias and enjoy the merry mixed crowd. *5pm-2am*

Generation Bar
 E1

At this popular place right in the middle of the St Georg gay strip the red light adds to the hazy mood – this is a smokers joint. *4pm-2am Sun-Thu, to 4am Fri & Sat*

Pick Up
26 D4

Sink into a leopard-print, glow-in-the-dark sofa and sip a martini under the raver-ready neon lights. Pick Up's kitschy, queer and proud of it. *3pm-1am*

Tom's Saloon
27 F6

Trust in Tom's to deliver the kink. St Georg's most renowned gay bar, established in 1974, flaunts a dark room, well-equipped play zones and DJ beats. Come dressed for theme nights (for example, in neon) to ensure entry. *8pm-2am, to 5am Sat & Sun*

Cocktail Bars

Bar Hamburg
 A3

A favourite haunt of A-list celebrities (Mick Jagger

and Claudia Schiffer have both passed through), Bar Hamburg has more than 70 whiskies, some 250 cocktails, and a cigar and shisha zone. Dress chic. *4pm-1am Sun-Thu, to 3am Fri & Sat*

Kyti Voo
 E1

A mixed crowd enjoys a menu of craft beer and cocktails until very late. At sunnier (or less dark) times, grab a table on the terrace. Cocktail happy hour is a particularly generous 5pm to 8pm daily. *5pm-late Mon-Sat, from 2pm Sun*

Pubs
Frau Möller
 E1

At this Lange Reihe institution outside tables wrap around the corner location and the kitchen stays open late. Food includes good German standards, and the wine and beer lists are the best you'll find at 5am. *11am-4am Mon-Thu, to 6am Fri & Sat, to 3am Sun*

Shopping
Speciality Shops
Blendwerk
31 **D2**

Stationery and gift-wrapping specialist Blendwerk has Leuchtturm notebooks and desk knick-knacks you never knew you needed; the latter especially make great keepsakes. *11am-7pm Mon-Fri, to 6pm Sat*

Chapeau St Georg
32 **E1**

Stylish toppers for special occasions (fascinators galore) as well as more traditional brimmed hats. *11am-6pm Mon-Sat*

Weinkauf St Georg
 D2

Small but knowledgeable Weinkauf St Georg showcases wines from Germany, France, Italy and Spain, although you might find the occasional bottle from further afield. *11am-7.30pm Mon-Fri, 10am-6pm Sat*

Atelier Figurart
 E3

At this studio for eccentric, theatrical handmade puppets and marionettes you can admire the display window (but please don't take photographs, as per the puppet-maker's wishes). *open by appointment*

Unique Souvenirs
Art of Hamburg
35 **D2**

Fun clothes, bags and other accessories with nautical colours and Hamburg slogans or other references make this a good place for cheerful souvenirs. *11am-7pm Mon-Sat*

Kaufhaus Hamburg
36 **D2**

Choose among everything from stationery and homewares to games and food for a great memento of your visit. *11am-7pm Mon-Fri, from 10am Sat*

See p100 for eating, drinking and shopping listings

Explore
Speicherstadt & HafenCity

Welcome to the waterfront, where old meets new. The Speicherstadt is the largest warehouse district in the world where the buildings stand on timber-pile foundations. A symbol of Hamburg, the seven-storey red-brick warehouses are today increasingly filled with fine museums. Crowned by the superlative Elbphilharmonie, HafenCity – an ongoing transformation – is Hamburg's most architecturally dynamic corner. Speicherstadt and HafenCity may have disparate origins (representing the city's oldest and newest regions), but they share an identity as a newly residential part of the town.

Getting Around

 **Walking**
Speicherstadt and HafenCity are an easy 10-minute walk south of the city centre.

 U-Bahn
The area is a short walk from Messberg U-Bahn station (line U1) or Baumwall (line U3). The U4 line links the Überseequartier stop in HafenCity to the rest of Hamburg.

Ferry
Speicherstadt is best explored on foot, but you can also reach the Elbphilharmonie from its ferry pier (Anleger Elbphilharmonie), located directly alongside the concert hall. Ferries travel between the Elbphilharmonie and Landungsbrücken (St Pauli) terminal.

THE BEST

CONCERT HALL
Elbphilharmonie (p89)

MINIATURE MUSEUM
Miniatur Wunderland (p88)

CHAMBER OF CURIOSITIES
Harry's Hamburger Hafenbasar & Museum (p95)

MARITIME HISTORY
Internationales Maritimes Museum (p87)

WAREHOUSE FOOD MARKET
Hobenköök (p96)

Internationales Maritimes Museum (p87)
SAIKO3P/SHUTTERSTOCK

SPEICHERSTADT & HAFENCITY

EXPLORE

Map Locations

- Deichstrasse
- Miniatur Wunderland
- HafenCity InfoCenter
- Spicy's Gewürzmuseum
- Harry's Hamburger Hafenbasar & Museum
- Hafenköök
- Poggenmühlen Brücke
- Oberhafen Kantine
- Kaffeemuseum Burg
- Dialoghaus
- Elbphilharmonie
- Speicherstadtmuseum
- Deutsches Zollmuseum
- Internationales Maritimes Museum

For more see
- Top Experiences ★ p87
- Experiences ★ p94
- Eating ✕ p100
- Drinking 🍷 p100
- Shopping 🛍 p101

0.2 miles / 400 m

★ TOP EXPERIENCE

Internationales Maritimes Museum

Hamburg is defined by its maritime past, and there's nowhere better to understand this fascinating history than the **Internationales Maritimes Museum** *(imm-hamburg.de; adult/reduced €21/13)*. Even if you're not into old ships, this place is worth a visit for its beautiful waterside location.

MAP MAP P86 **D3**

Early Maritime History
Considered the world's largest private collection of nautical treasures, the museum houses 26,000 model ships, 50,000 construction plans, 5000 illustrations, 2000 films, 1.5 million photographs and much more. Don't miss the exhibit on the early stages of humankind's 3000-year marine fascination. Ancient navigational devices, rudimentary communication systems and models of vessels belonging to civilisations from the Phoenicians to the Vikings are an astonishing journey through seafaring history. Don't miss the 1657 Dutch *Atlantis Majoris,* the first-ever nautical atlas.

Kaispeicher B
It's apt that this terrific collection inhabits what is believed to be Hamburg's oldest waterfront warehouse, the **Kaispeicher B**. Built in 1878 as a grain silo, the 10-storey structure, with its neo-Gothic gables and cornices, would come to represent the prevailing style in 19th-century Hamburg and the Hanseatic ports beyond. Amid new construction taking place all around, the Kaispeicher B is an important anchor to the past.

Shipbuilding
The exhibition on the mechanics of shipbuilding and how it's changed over the centuries is a must-see. The story begins with dugout canoes, including a millennia-old hollowed-out tree trunk found nearby.

PLANNING TIP
Allow a good half-day to do the extensive exhibition justice. Wandering through the collection for a quick overview and then going back to what's of particular interest is a good strategy.

Scan this QR code for info on guided tours.

★ TOP EXPERIENCE

Miniatur Wunderland

Even the worst cynics are quickly transformed into fans of this vast **miniature wonderland** *(miniatur-wunderland.de; adult/child €20/12.50)*. Let out your inner child: prepare to gasp at the world's largest model railway and see a mini A380 swoop out of the sky and land at a fully functional miniature airport.

MAP P86 **B3**

PLANNING TIP
On weekends and during summer holidays, pre-purchase admission online to skip the ticketing queues. Come early, as lines form to get up front at the exhibits.

Hamburg

The highlight of the whole collection (apart from the airport) is the reconstruction of Hamburg. Everything from the port to the church steeples is almost perfectly rendered, with automated trains and other vehicles zipping around it all. Note the impressive **Millerntor-Stadion**, where SV Hamburger is beating St Pauli 3–0 (not by coincidence).

Europe & Beyond

The main exhibition floor also takes in Scandinavia (Narvik and Kiruna), Austria, the US (where Las Vegas segues effortlessly into Miami Beach), Middle Germany and Knuffingen – a recreated German town.

Follow Switzerland down the mountain and past the chocolate factory to the floor below, where all manner of European scenes are on show, including Venice and Rome (complete with Trevi Fountain). Dioramas give quick overviews of German history.

Don't miss the control room, a large bank of televisions that would make NASA proud.

Knuffingen Airport

For many, the exhibition's biggest highlight is how planes take over from trains at the vast Knuffingen Airport in miniature. Planes taxi, take off and land, and there's even a crashed plane, with flames, smoke and fire engines rushing to the scene.

Scan this QR code for the museum's excellent YouTube channel.

★ TOP EXPERIENCE

Elbphilharmonie

The **Elbphilharmonie** *(elbphilharmonie.de),* perched majestically over the Elbe River, is one of Europe's most exciting and recent architectural feats. Framed over a restored historic brick warehouse, its striking glass design rises high above the skyline. Inside, the one-of-a-kind concert hall boasts exceptional acoustics and immersive surprises.

MAP P86 **A4**

Architecture & History
The Elbphilharmonie ('Elphi' for short) arrived late and well over budget (p97). But what an end result. It's essentially two buildings in one. The bottom half is a converted brick warehouse whose facade is largely unchanged; it stored cocoa, tea and tobacco until the 1990s. Sitting atop the warehouse, on its own foundations, is a soaring edifice of more than 1000 curved glass panels. It was all designed by Swiss architectural firm Herzog & de Meuron, who drew their inspiration for the project from three very different structures: tents, sports stadiums and the Ancient Greek theatre at Delphi. The building's iconic glass design with its wave-like roof is meant to mimic the ethereal, floating quality of the maritime element, from a billowing sail to the movement of water.

Entrance
From street level, the 82m-long escalator is the first sign that the interior is every bit as special as the world-famous facade. Said to be the longest escalator in Europe, it's a long, slightly curved golden tube. Riding it is like traversing a tunnel of magical bubbles.

PLANNING TIP
To take an excellent photograph of the Elbphilharmonie with red-brick warehouses in the foreground, head to **Holzbrücke**, a short distance north.

Scan this QR code to book free Plaza tickets (and skip the ticket-office queue).

DIMITAR12/SHUTTERSTOCK

QUICK BREAK
Right across from the entrance, **Carls Brasserie** (p100) serves French bistro snacks. There's a restaurant and cafe inside the Elphi, but if you want to stretch your legs there's endless gastronomy along **Deichstrasse** (p47), a 15-minute walk away.

Plaza & Viewing Platform

Atop the escalators, and negotiated via a series of Escher-like stairways, the Plaza has a shop, restaurants and the hotel entrance. Be sure to head for the balcony to take in the wrap-around **viewing platform** *(free)*: there are splendid vistas at every turn.

Concert Hall

The concert hall and other performance spaces – the building's raison d'être – are arguably the best in the world. Acoustically the concert hall is the most advanced in existence. The programme is diverse, and there are at least a few shows every week; tickets go for as little as €20. Advance bookings are recommended.

The **Grand Hall** is the main space for large-scale events such as symphony and opera. 'Vineyard'-inspired seating ripples down around the centre stage in multilevel, terrace-like steps, offering unobstructed views throughout. Seamlessly integrated across walls and ceilings, the Elphi's state-of-the-art acoustics system, White Skin, comprises 10,000 individually shaped gypsum-fibre panels evenly dispersing sound. The concept was designed by master acoustician Yasuhisa Toyota. Peek behind you to see a custom-built organ with 4765 pipes blending into the back wall like a chameleon.

The Elbphilharmonie's trifecta of performance venues includes two more much smaller spaces. The 550-seat **Recital Hall** hosts chamber music, jazz and soloists between wavy, wood-panelled interiors (another sound-dispersing innovation). Last but not least, the 150-seat **Kaistudios** doesn't typically put on concerts but holds interactive workshops introducing traditional instruments from other cultures or fiddling around with modular synthesizers. Participatory art projects also take place on occasion; check the website for upcoming offerings.

MUSICAL HERITAGE

After you visit the Elbphilharmonie, discover orchestra history around Neustadt's **Komponisten-Quartier** (p62) and live-music venues along the Reeperbahn's **Grosse Freiheit** (p125) to understand Hamburg's truly polyphonic musical pedigree.

PORT ANNIVERSARY

The Elphi is the centrepiece of Hamburg's port anniversary in early May. During the three-day celebration concerts are shown on a gigantic screen above the venue's steps, creating an amphitheatre-like atmosphere.

🚶 WALKING TOUR
Where Speicherstadt Meets HafenCity

Constructed between 1883 and 1927, Speicherstadt is the world's largest warehouse district built on timber-pile foundations. Museums and restaurants now occupy the warehouses and red-brick buildings that made up a once frenetic free port. Old Speicherstadt demurely neighbours the new HafenCity development. On this walk, discover what these twin neighborhoods are about.

START	END	LENGTH
Elbphilharmonie	Hobenköök	1.7km; 30 minutes

1 Sublime Concert Hall

Take Europe's longest escalator up to the 360-degree outdoor viewing terrace at the **Elbphilharmonie** (p89). With encompassing views of Speicherstadt and HafenCity (and other areas too), this is the perfect place to start.

2 Museum of Trade

To see where Speicherstadt comes from, locals visit this century-old warehouse, transformed into the **Speicherstadtmuseum** (p94) and housing exhibitions on Hamburg's trading past. Sometimes you can catch demonstrations on the trade in tea or coffee too.

3 Maritime Collection

On a permanently docked vessel, the **Hafenbasar** (Harbour Bazaar; p95) is Hamburg's most eccentric museum. A sailor's collection of over 300,000 dusty oddities are a testament to a port city's worldly curiosity.

4 Scaled-down City

Miniatur Wunderland (p88) museum has lots to admire, including the world's largest model railway. Its highly detailed, fully functional replica of the Port of Hamburg is enchanting. Working container terminals, cranes, and cargo ships are scale-rendered and autonomous with real-time tracking – and provide a little insight into the logistics business today.

5 Model Hamburg

Head to the **HafenCity Info-Center** (p95) for a peek at an intricate architectural model of a 2030 Hamburg and a full perspective on the waterfront area. You're looking at the future of the city – only half of what's shown currently exists.

6 Treasures of the Deep

On your way further into Hafen-City (amid landscapes still very much in development), the **Internationales Maritimes Museum** (p87) is worth a stop. In a 10-storey former shipping warehouse you can see the world's largest private collection of maritime treasures.

7 Bridge with a View

The **Poggenmühlen Brücke** (Poggenmühlen Bridge) offers the perfect scenic perspective on Speicherstadt in all its glory. Be sure to take a snap here.

8 Market Stop

At **Hobenköök** (p96), a sprawling freight warehouse turned market hall, relax and unwind with a coffee or a bite. It's a 10-minute walk from Poggenmühlen Bridge (or a couple of minutes by e-scooter).

EXPERIENCES

Delve into History at Speicherstadtmuseum   MUSEUM

MAP: ① P86 B3

A century-old warehouse is the atmospheric backdrop for exhibitions on Hamburg's trading past at the **Speicherstadtmuseum** *(shmh.de/speicherstadtmuseum; adult/child €5/free)*. When Hamburg signed up to the German Reich in 1871, so joining the German Customs Federation, a separate free port became necessary – and so the Speicherstadt was born. An older neighbourhood was demolished, displacing 24,000 people, to make room for Speicherstadt construction from 1885 to 1927. This area was spared wartime destruction, and in 2015 it made UNESCO's World Heritage list in recognition of its historic role in rapidly expanding global trade.

The museum's immersive displays delve into the life, work and trade that shaped the world's largest ever warehouse complex. Exhibits highlight goods once stored there, such as coffee, tea, cocoa and spices, as well as tools, documents and photographs related to dockworkers, merchants and port business.

Enjoy the Best View of the Speicherstadt   PANORAMIC OUTLOOK

MAP: ② P86 E2

The seven-storey red-brick warehouses lining the Speicherstadt archipelago stretch all the way to Baumwall, making up the world's largest continuous warehouse complex. Their neo-Gothic gables and (mostly) green copper roofs are reflected in the narrow canals of this free-port zone. Historic boats line the waterways.

Stand on the **Poggenmühlen Brücke** for the most comprehensive view of it all and take a few photos at sunset.

Walk Around the HafenCity Development   URBAN REJUVENATION

MAP: ③ P86 B3

The Speicherstadt merges into Europe's biggest inner-city urban development, **HafenCity**. A long derelict port area of 155 hectares is being redeveloped to add restaurants, shops, apartments, schools and offices. In the next 20 years it's anticipated that some 12,000 people will live in the district and 40,000 people will work here. For now, with only some projects complete and large swathes of land still vacant, the effect can be bleak, but the vision is impressive. The district integrates energy-efficient buildings, green mobility solutions and extensive public spaces, aiming to create a modern, climate-resilient area in the former port.

See Hamburg's 'Model Perspective'   REVEALING DIORAMA

With a red-brick facade, the *Kesselhaus* (Old Boiler House) looks like a smaller, stockier version of the Speicherstadt warehouses. It houses the **HafenCity InfoCenter** (MAP: 4 P86 B3; *hafencity.com/infocenter, closed Mon*), worth a quick stop not just for the maps, pamphlets and tips from HafenCity tourism experts but also for a look at its gigantic scale model of Hamburg. Measuring 8m by 4m and constructed at a 1:500 scale, the architectural model is incredibly detailed, with pint-sized yet intricate installations of the Elbphilharmonie and other waterfront restorations. This is not a model of today's Hamburg but rather a full representation of the city once development plans are completed. Only about 50% of what's shown in the model exists right now; the expectation is that by 2030 these dreams will have become a reality.

Visit Hamburg's Most Eccentric Museum

CHAMBER OF CURIOSITIES

Climb aboard if you dare –

Harry's Hamburger Hafenbasar & Museum (MAP: 5 P86 B3; *hafenbasar.de; adult/child €5/3*) is an exhibit not for the claustrophobic, asthmatic or easily queasy.

On a permanently docked vessel, the *Hafenbasar* (Harbour Bazaar) is a *Wunderkammer* (chamber of curiosities). The museum began in 1952 as a place for sailor Harry Rosenberg (1925–2000) to display oddities collected on his seafaring travels. Today it's packed to the rafters with over 300,000 items you've probably never seen (or heard of) before. Harry's has even inspired a song by Tom Waits.

Initiation masks, voodoo dolls, tribal penis protectors, animal and human bones and pirate weapons are just a few items dustily displayed across 33 labyrinthine rooms. Two (real) shrunken human heads sit behind a wall with a warning sign.

Watch your head and take allergy meds before entering. The *Hafenbasar* is open Saturday and Sunday. Some interesting souvenirs from West Africa and beyond are on hand, too.

🌐 ANCHORING SUSTAINABILITY

When it comes to climate change, Hamburg has more to lose than most European cities. Much of its landmass lies just 6m above sea level, and any increase in global temperatures will have a catastrophic impact. Even without rising sea levels, Hamburg's position on the Elbe River and its proximity to the North Sea make it especially vulnerable to extreme weather. Enter HafenCity's model for sustainable urban development. Necessity certainly plays a role, but the district is also being reshaped by Hamburg's progressive spirit. Through HafenCity, Hamburg's urban planners have a firm eye on a more liveable, resilient future.

Dine Farm to Table at Hobenköök
WAREHOUSE MARKET HALL

MAP: 6 P86 F3

Jiving with Hamburg's HafenCity rejuvenation, freight warehouse **Hobenköök** *(hobenkoeoek.de; free, closed Sun & Mon)* has been reimagined as a hipster market. Since 2013 the old railway logistics hall has become a vibrant cultural and gastronomic experience, spotlighting regional, sustainable produce from local farmers, fishers and artisans. The on-site restaurant-canteen features breakfast and lunch specials, salads and cakes. The venue also hosts cooking classes and artisan food workshops.

See Through Sound at the Dialoghaus
EXPERIMENTAL EXHIBITION

MAP: 7 P86 E2

Hamburg's **Dialoghaus** *(Dialogue House; dialog-in-hamburg.de; adult/child €24.50/18.50, closed Mon)* provides a powerful simulation of what daily life is like for people with impaired vision. During the one-hour tour, visitors walk through completely dark rooms with their guides, taking on everyday scenarios like crossing a street or shopping. Dialogue House is part of a global initiative that began in Hamburg and has since expanded to many countries; the non-profit also puts on dinner-in-the-dark nights.

Dine on Northern German Food in a Historic Building
LEANING RESTAURANT

Since 1925 the brick restaurant **Oberhafen Kantine** (MAP: 8 P86 F2), beneath a train bridge, has served up an array of traditional Hamburg fare. Here you can order a Hamburger and get the real thing: a patty made with onions and various seasonings. Roast beef and fish round out a trip back to the days when the surrounding piers echoed to the shouts of seafarers. The outdoor tables are the comfiest choice, but you'll need to book those ahead. You'll notice

ELBTOWER PROGRESS

In the HafenCity InfoCenter, on the future Hamburg scale model, you'll see a northeastern building standing well above the rest. The Elbtower might one day be Hamburg's tallest building and Germany's third tallest. It presently stands at 100m, only about 40% of its planned final height of 245m (for comparison, the Elbphilharmonie is 110m). Construction was halted in October 2023 when the original developer filed for insolvency. Since then the project has remained on hold. At research time, negotiations to take over the €950-million project were underway. An information board at the InfoCenter provides greater detail on the Elbtower vision.

ELBPHILHARMONIE CONTROVERSY

Construction of the Elbphilharmonie, was scheduled to take place from 2007 to 2010 but actually took until 2017 which certainly got people talking. Once the building was finally completed, controversy over delays and cost overruns died down, with many Hamburgers enjoying the plaudits and glamour the project brought to the city. Still, concerns remain that officials have prioritised signature infrastructure projects over more pressing issues such as public housing. After all, the Elbphilharmonie came in five times over its initial budget of €200 million and went six years past its intended completion date.

---

the building has a slight tilt – it's because water has eroded its foundations over the years.

Discover Hamburg's Coffee Exchange   TRADE HISTORY

Coffee has a direct and rich connection to Hamburg's maritime past. From the mid-19th century until well into the 20th century, this was the world's coffee-trading centre and the main entry hub for coffee into Europe.

The *Kaffee-Börse* (Coffee Exchange) opened in 1887. Just as New York and London shaped futures markets for other commodities, it quickly became the reference point for international coffee pricing. Merchants, brokers and shipping firms in Hamburg set global trends and standards for the trade in coffee.

At the **Kaffeemuseum Burg** (MAP: 9 P86 D2; *kaffeemuseum-burg.de; with audioguide €9, closed Mon*) you can discover coffee history through one of the city's oldest family-run coffee companies.

The collection is based on Burg Coffee Roasters' antique roasting machines, grinders, brewing equipment and documents detailing the bean's journey through importation, roasting and consumption.

Considering so much of Speicherstadt was built to store coffee beans, the museum's location is apt: it's in a converted red-brick warehouse building.

Savour Exotic Spices with a Dash of History   SPICE MUSEUM

The Speicherstadt warehouse district was designed specifically for storing imported goods such as coffee, tea, tobacco and spices and shipping them all around Europe. So while **Spicy's Gewürzmuseum** (MAP: 10 P86 B3, *Spice's Museum of Spices; spicys.de; adult/family €7/15*) might sound like a bizarre attraction for a German city (a country known for its aversion to seasoning), this museum dedicated to spices and herbs fits perfectly with Hamburg's harbour history.

BEST SPEICHERSTADT EXPERIENCES ON A BUDGET

Elbphilharmonie Plaza
MAP: P86 **A4**

Outside the concert hall, grab a free ticket and ride Europe's longest escalator to the 37m-high, 360-degree viewing platform. Stay on the balcony as long as you like. The Plaza (p90) is open daily. *10am-midnight, last entry 11.30pm*

Baakenpark
MAP: **11** P86 **F4**

A green haven in HafenCity; with weekend concerts and even an occasional open-air cinema, it's a lovely place to (mostly) escape the neighbourhood's cranes and construction. *24hr*

Harry's Hamburger Hafenbasar & Museum
see **5** P86 **B3**

Harry's 'Chamber of Curiosities' costs just a fiver to enter and promises a memorable experience for multiple reasons – disbelief, fascination and claustrophobia, among others.

In a historic warehouse you can embark on a flavour-packed journey through global spice cultivation and trade across more than 900 exhibits. Spices, herbs and rare seasonings can be touched, smelled and sampled during a deeply immersive olfactory experience; each one has a connection to the city's port industry days. Discover 'grains of paradise' (tiny West African seeds with a spicy citrus taste) and Cubeb pepper, known as 'tailed pepper', a slightly bitter ingredient once well used in medieval Europe.

Learn to Decode Food Labels at the Additives Museum FOOD SCIENCE MUSEUM

Hamburg's long history of engineering and trade-driven innovation has fostered science museums with oddball, anti-textbook flair.

The **Deutsches Zusatzstoffmuseum** (MAP: **12** P86 **F4**; *German Food Additives Museum; adult/child €3.50/free, closed Sun - Tues*) sheds light on the unhealthy artificial additives hidden in our meals. Founded by the Hamburg Food Foundation, it's a real eye-opener that reveals how additives are snuck onto labels in unexpected ways. The exhibit is in German; use a translation app.

Just on the outskirts of HafenCity, the **Medizinhistorisches Museum** is a showcase of medical instruments and wax moulages hidden within the University Teaching Hospital. It's a 15-minute tram ride from Oberhafenbrücke or only five minutes by bicycle or e-scooter – just take the bridge over Oberhafen Kantine (p96).

A CITY OF MERCHANTS

Hamburg's commercial character was forged in 1189, when Emperor Friedrich I (Barbarossa) granted the city free trading rights and a customs duty exemption. This transformed the former missionary settlement and 9th-century moated fortress of Hammaburg into an important Hanseatic League port. The city prospered until 1842, when the Great Fire destroyed a third of its buildings. In WWII 80% of Hamburg's port and 40% of its industry were reduced to rubble. The postwar resurgence is an economic miracle. Alongside its famous harbour, its media industry is a strength – most large German publications are produced here.

Unwind in Unexpected HafenCity Greenery   URBAN PARK

On the southeastern reaches of HafenCity, **Baakenpark** (see 11 P86 F4) is proof that the development isn't only commercial space and construction sites. Unfolding seemingly endlessly across a 1.6-hectare artificial peninsula, the park is particularly family-friendly, with playgrounds and picnic spots under cherry trees, and a soccer field.

Assess Port Duties at the German Customs Museum   TRADE & TAX HISTORY

The **Deutsches Zollmuseum** (MAP: 13 P86 D2; *German Customs Museum; adult/child €2/free*) offers an immersive journey through the history and modern-day operations of customs regulation in Hamburg and Germany more generally.

In the atmospheric Kornhausbrücke customs office, the museum traces the early days of trading under the Ancient Romans, who were largely responsible for setting up taxation and customs checkpoints in Europe, and runs to the present day of German and European regulation.

The highlights include exhibits on smuggling and the museum ship *Oldenburg*, which is permanently moored outside. You can board the 1976-commissioned vessel, which formerly patrolled the North Sea for environmental protection; it was also responsible for smuggling prevention and rescues.

LISTINGS

Best Places for...

€ Budget €€ Midrange €€€ Top End

See p86 for map of locations

Eating

Truly Hamburg Dining

Fleetschlösschen €€
14 D2

Overlook a Speicherstadt canal while savouring northern German–style fish dishes with cucumber salad and remoulade. Limited indoor seats, brilliant outdoor seating. *11am-10pm*

Casual Lunch

Carls Brasserie €€
15 A4

Facing the Elbphilharmonie, this casual place offers predominantly French cuisine, such as *croque-monsieur* and other toasts in the bistro, with a little more sophistication in the brasserie. The bistro offers better value. *noon-11pm*

Strauchs Falco €€
16 D3

The menu here is astonishingly broad (tapas, pizza, pasta, seafood) without compromising on quality. Its speciality is flame-grilled meats. *noon-3pm & 5.30pm-midnight Mon-Fri, 12.30pm-midnight Sat & Sun*

Fine Dining

Bootshaus Grill & Bar €€€
17 B4

Steaks in all their glory dominate proceedings here. Choose your eat and preferred sauce and you're guaranteed to be as happy as a clam. *noon-3pm & 6-10pm Tue-Sat*

Table €€€
18 E3

Lauded young German chef Kevin Fehling serves haute cuisine on a communal single table at this beautiful modern-build dining room. Sustainable, experimental dishes echo the restaurant's location in futuristic HafenCity. *7pm-midnight Tue-Sat*

Drinking

Cafes

Kaffeemuseum Burg
see **9** D2

Hamburg's coffee museum has a cafe that's open to the public – there's no requirement to visit the exhibition. Baristas serve brews from Burg Coffee Roasters, a Hamburg family business founded in 1923; the museum houses a collection of its antique coffee-making equipment. *10am-6pm*

Speicherstadt Coffee Roastery
19 B3

Speicherstadt's legacy as the site of Hamburg's 'coffee exchange' lives on at this slick, modern caffeinated paradise. As if the house-roasted brews weren't enough, there's also a tantalising cake selection. *10am-6pm*

Speicherstadt Coffee Roastery
WERNER SPREMBERG/SHUTTERSTOCK

Kaffeeklappe at Speicherstadtmuseum
see B3

Stop in for a delectable coffee made from house-roasted beans at this cute, unpretentious cafe in the warehouse museum. The Kaffeeklappe (once a word for quick coffee stalls catering to maritime workers) has excellent cake too. *10am-6pm*

Shopping

Boutiques

Hafen-Spezerei
20 D3

Your one-stop shop for gourmet treats from around the region, including speciality coffee and tea from local Hamburg businesses – perfectly fitting for the area's historic trade roots. *10am-7pm Mon-Sat*

Kuestensilber Concept Store
21 A1

At fashion designer and goldsmith Clementine Schmodde's boutique you'll find maritime-inspired jewellery with dainty shells and anchors, plus scented candles, perfumes and more surprises. Photography by her husband, Leif, is also for sale. *11am-7pm*

Explore
St Pauli & the Reeperbahn

St Pauli is Hamburg's alternative darling. The neighbourhood's buzzy creativity and rougher edges give Hamburg nuance. When markets take over the central Spielbudenplatz square there are few finer places to be – smack-dab in the middle of the Reeperbahn action or not. Exploring St Pauli after dark might mean you'll never go home again: all-nighter parties pulse across legendary *Kneipen* (dive pubs) and underground clubs occupy such spaces as a WWII bunker and a smugglers' prison. After nightlife drains St Pauli's energy, daytimes can be haggard – but Sunday mornings are worth rising early (or staying up late) to visit the famous Fischmarkt.

Getting Around

 **Walking**

Roaming aimlessly is how you ride the St Pauli roller-coaster – short, off Reeperbahn side streets are made for stumbling upon surprises. Mind broken glass, pickpockets and sticky surfaces.

 **S-Bahn & U-Bahn**

Getting here is easy. The Reeperbahn S-Bahn station (receiving lines S1, S2 and S3) is in the heart of the action in front of Grosse Freiheit. St Pauli U-Bahn station (U3) intersects with the Reeperbahn S-Bahn station. Feldtrasse (U3) is northern Hamburg's key stop.

 Ferry

Commuter ferries stop next to the Fischmarkt.

Christmas Market (p118), Spielbudenplatz
MIKHAIL MARKOVSKIY/SHUTTERSTOCK

THE BEST

LEGENDARY MARKET
Fischmarkt (p106)

FLEA MARKET
Flohschanze (p116)

BURLESQUE SHOWS
Bunny Burlesque (p116)

DIVE BAR
Zur Ritze (p117)

INDIE ROCK CLUB
Molotow (p120)

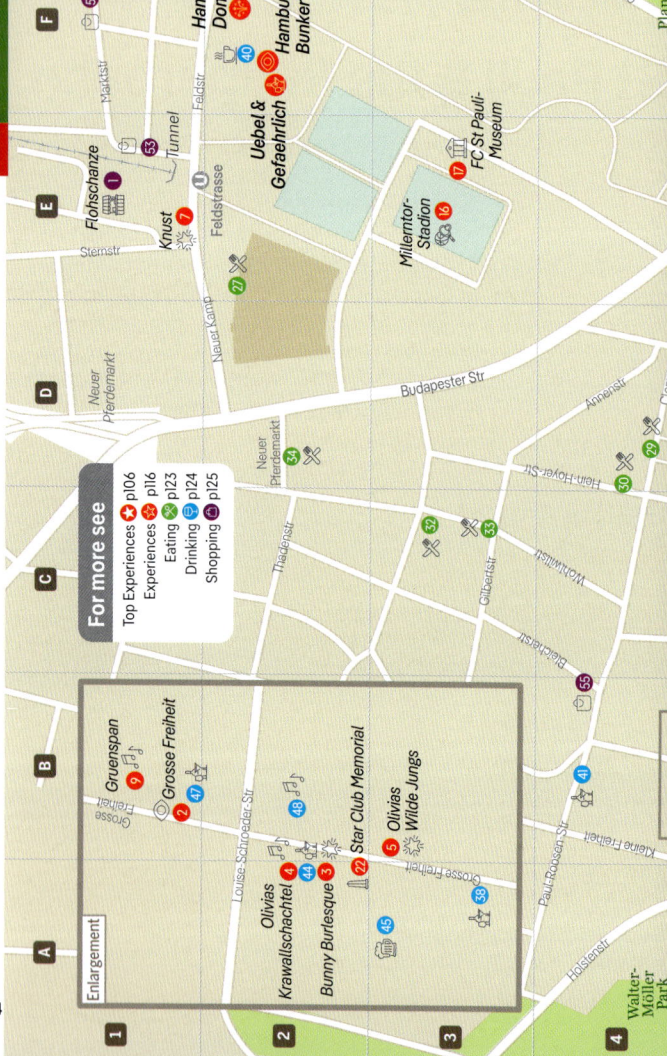

ST PAULI & THE REEPERBAHN

EXPLORE

- Grosse Wallanlagen
- Millerntorplatz
- Elbpark
- St Pauli
- Clouds
- Tanzende Türme
- Mojo Club
- Kleine Seilerstr
- Detlev-Bremer-Str
- Simon-von-Utrecht-Str
- Japster Str
- Beim Trichter
- Zirkusweg
- Kastanienallee
- Hopfenstr
- Seewartenstr
- Landungsbrücken
- Helgoländer Allee
- St Pauli Nachtmarkt
- Taubenstr
- Spielbudenplatz
- St Pauli Christmas Market
- Docks Prinzenbar
- St-Pauli-Hafenstr
- St Pauli Harbour
- Frau Hedi
- Davidstr
- Hans-Albers-Platz
- Friedrichstr
- Harbertstr
- Gerhardstr
- Bernhard-Nocht-Str
- StrandPauli
- Hamburger Berg
- Zur Ritze
- Talstr
- Querstr
- Silbersackstr
- Balduinstr
- Erichstr
- Elbe River
- Reeperbahn
- Bertha-Keyser-Weg
- Friedrichstr
- Silbersackstwiete
- Antonistr
- St-Pauli-Fischmarkt
- Beatles-Platz
- See Enlargement
- Grosse Freiheit
- Molotow
- Lincolnstr
- Park Fiction
- Nobistor
- Reeperbahn
- Königstr
- Silbersackstr
- Fischerhaus
- Fischmarkt
- Breite Str
- Sandtorhafen

0.1 miles / 200 m

Tunnel

★ **TOP EXPERIENCE**

Fischmarkt

A port tradition since 1703, the legendary **Fischmarkt** draws over 70,000 people. Whether or not you're a morning person, it's an energising, one-of-a-kind sunrise experience. Get caught up in the tidal wave of high-sensory shenanigans, from the clamour of vendors to the clatter of fish grilling.

MAP P104 **A8**

PLANNING TIP
Take the bus from Hamburg Hauptbahnhof to have more time at the market (it's always crowded). Afterwards you can stroll along the **Elbmeile promenade** (p130) back to the inner city.

Harbour History

Hamburg's Fischmarkt has been a vital part of the city's maritime culture since the early 18th century. What started as a simple outdoor marketplace where fishers could dock and sell fresh catches directly to customers has evolved into a cultural landmark. Today it's one of the most evocative sights for business and pleasure amid seafaring history.

Seafood Smorgasboard

If Hamburg's techno clubs aren't convincing enough, the Fischmarkt is a perfect excuse to pull a Saturday all-nighter. On Sunday mornings, vendors sprawl across the riverbanks churning out fresh seafood delicacies for early risers and the hungover masses. The iconic specialties are the *Fischbrötchen* (fish sandwiches) topped with decadent North Sea and Elbe River delights. The assortment is incredible: pickled herring, smoked salmon, fried or grilled fish fillets, regional shrimp or crab – you name it. Catches are packed onto German bread rolls (crusty on the outside, soft on the inside) and served hot or cold. Toppings depend on the seller and allow for some creativity; possibilities include raw onions, pickles, lettuce and remoulade or horseradish sauce. Every stand serves the sandwiches a little differently. The best way to

NOPPASIN WONGCHUM/SHUTTERSTOCK

choose is to look at what others are having. Fish sandwiches have been a Hamburg delicacy since the mid-19th century, when bustling port commerce led to a demand for quick, portable meals. Enjoy yours at a standing table or on the go. On slightly cool riverside mornings, it's a perfect breakfast.

Fresh Produce

Back in the day, fishmongers auctioned their wares in a fast-paced, noisy manner to attract buyers. Today *Marktschreier* (market criers) keep this bartering tradition alive and are the undisputed stars of the Fischmarkt. Vendors artfully arrange their produce – bananas, cherries, kumquats and whatever else is on hand that week – and boisterously present it to the crowds with a circus ringmaster's flair.

QUICK BREAK
Up the hill and spilling onto a quiet St Pauli square, **Cafe Geyer** (p124) is a lovely spot for sitting down and escaping the crowds. Hang around until the market dies down.

TIME IS OF THE ESSENCE

Arrive as early as you can to watch the sun rise over the harbour. If you're walking to the Fish Auction Hall, allow extra time to fight through crowds. Score the best deals in the market's last 30 minutes (9am to 9.30am), when vendors would rather slash prices than lug extra wares home. After 9.30am, only a few vendors (mostly souvenirs and clothing) continue.

Scan this QR code for the auction hall's music programme.

Some sell *Wundertuete* (surprise bags; €15 to €20). These are prepacked bulk deals with a bit of everything already sorted into shopping bags. There's no trading those items – what's inside is what you get. Some produce comes directly from farms, but mostly it's sourced from wholesalers. Bring cash. Sales happen quickly, and many vendors don't have card machines.

Fish Auction Hall

Inaugurated in 1896, the historic **Fish Auction Hall** is a testament to Hamburg's maritime heritage. While the building once hosted fish auctions, today it's a venue for live entertainment, which runs from 6am till noon on market days. Consider German pop singers and rock cover bands your wake-up call.

The hall itself is an architectural charmer. From both inside and out, if you look closely enough, you'll see how the building was modelled after a Roman basilica (a three-nave layout with a central crossing and dome, high ceilings and side aisles). A steel framework, brickwork and an iron-and-glass vaulted roof imbue a spiritually inspired facade with industrial character. Once upon a time a large bridge allowed up to eight steamships at once to unload wares directly inside. This feature, as well as many other parts of the structure, was severely damaged during WWII.

Plant Auction

Next to the Fish Auction Hall, the plant auction from the truck of the **Hoellanderischer Bluemenkonig** (Dutch Flower King) is not to be missed. Locals flock to this lively bartering spot hoping to score excellent deals on flora from olive trees to potted perennials. Watch as greenery and wads of cash change hands at breakneck speed.

⭐ **TOP EXPERIENCE**

Hamburg Bunker

Rising from the northern reaches of St Pauli, the **Hamburg Bunker**, a WWII air-raid shelter, was transformed in 2024 into a panoramic cultural attraction. Climb a cement-poured 'mountain path' to a rooftop urban garden offering 360-degree views across the city. Best of all, it's free to visit.

MAP P104 **F2**

Flakturm IV

Conceived in the early 1940s as part of a Germany-spanning bunker-building programme, the monumental **Flakturm IV** (Flak Tower) was a critical part of the Nazis' plan to unveil Hamburg as the 'Führer's City'. Up to 1000 forced labourers from occupied areas toiled in inhumane conditions during the gigantic building's construction.

Ironically, the culmination of their work was a bunker protecting German civilians from Allied bombardment. The tower was used most frequently at the end of WWII. Around 18,000 people could shelter here behind 3.5m-thick walls that also housed two towers, one for combat and weapons and the other a radio station.

Cultural Epicentre

Though it is a gargantuan, painful reminder of the Nazi era, Flakturm IV was never slated for demolition. Apart from other considerations, bringing down the immense structure would likely damage surrounding residential buildings. During the postwar years the bunker became headquarters for a jumble of creative endeavours from media companies to the Ensemble Resonanz, a unique

PLANNING TIP
The bunker is located next to the Feldstrasse train station. After your visit, walk around St Pauli to take in the neighbourhood's local life.

FELIX GERINGSWALD/SHUTTERSTOCK

TAKE A BREAK
Next to the bunker, the **Rindermarkthalle** (p123) is a modernised market hall featuring a food court-like area with stands serving everything from authentic Italian pizza to Vietnamese pho.

string group known for experimental classical performances. Today the bunker's five floors are home to a **hotel** and the Constant Grind (p124) coffee shop and boast incredible panoramas of the city. The best reason to head up, though, is for the exciting urban gardening project at the very top.

Mountain Path

The bunker's 'mountain path' is a spiralling **staircase** winding around the building's exterior all the way to the rooftop garden. The entire 560m-long, 60m-high ascent comprises around 300 steps.

It's best to take it slowly, as there's much to see along the way. Signage details the bunker's history, and you'll probably want to savour the scenic views along the way. Down below, the neighbouring Millerntor-Stadion, a 30,000-capacity soccer stadium that's the home ground of FC St Pauli, might be buzzing during team practice or even booming with a game. Also look out for the postwar functionalist design of Hamburg's TV Tower. At 271.5m, this is Hamburg's tallest building, though it's been closed to the public since 2001.

Rooftop Garden

The initiative of a local residents' non-profit, the rooftop garden is an impressive example of sustainable urban development. Here the Hamburg Bunker showcases how even the most gigantic of concrete jungles can incorporate the green of nature. **Hilldegarden** is in every sense a leafy oasis. Over 20,000 trees and other verdant flora adorn 10,000 sq metres of rooftop space. From here, bustling St Pauli seems very far away and spectacular 360-degree views sweep across the city. Grab a beverage from the garden bar-kiosk and stay awhile to relax in one of the many lawn chairs.

Evil & Dangerous

Hamburg Bunker holds yet one more secret: a 1000-person-strong, delirium-inducing nightclub for trance and techno raves. At **Uebel & Gefährlich** (MAP P104 F2; *Evil & Dangerous; uebelundgefaehrlich.com*), DJ sets, live music and parties rock the soundproof bunker. Situated on the building's 4th floor, the venue opens for special events only. Check its website for the full schedule. Uebel & Gefaehrlich's eclectic cultural events span everything from punk rock to stand-up comedy, hip-hop and international bands. Some events sell out; buy tickets beforehand via the website.

CARNIVAL FUN
Founded in 1329, the month-long **Hamburger Dom** (MAP P104 F2) is Germany's largest pop-up amusement park. It's held in March, July and November, and each season carouses differently. For example, in winter there's *Glühwein* (mulled wine). Hit the temporary fairgrounds on **Heiligengeistfeld** (adjacent to the Hamburg Bunker) for a truly German carnival experience – roller-coasters, traditional games like tin-can throwing and beer tents.

WALKING TOUR

St Pauli by Day

Few neighbourhoods in Europe swagger quite like St Pauli. But beyond its brashness and bright lights, the area does have an identity that defines it – one of solidarity, openness to all and an ability to provide something for everyone. All across the neighbourhood, quintessential haunts, diverse as they are, capture that spirit.

START	END	LENGTH
Hamburg Bunker	Indra Club	1.3km; 20 minutes

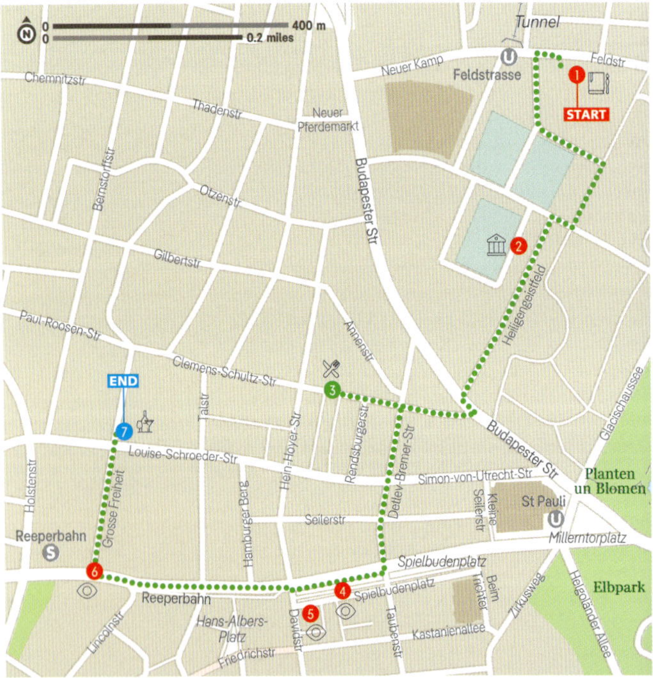

1. Garden-topped WWII Relic

Jutting into the sky, the **Hamburg Bunker** (p109) is an unmissable St Pauli landmark. Climb the stairs for some WWII history, satisfying city-wide views and – the best part – a relaxing rooftop garden.

2. Football Museum

Located at the Millerntor-Stadion, and run by fans and volunteers, the **FC St Pauli-Museum** (p119) celebrates St Pauli's beloved football team in all its unique, unconventional glory. Exhibits tell a vibrant story about the fandom's anti-establishment, countercultural spirit.

3. Local Haunt

At **Café Mimosa** (p123), a gem of a neighbourhood cafe, you can relax inside among theatrical flourishes or grab a table outside. It's a great place to plot further exploration of the surrounding streets.

4. Charismatic Square

In the heart of the neighbourhood, offbeat square **Spielbudenplatz** (p117) is where the Reeperbahn red-light district transitions into a vibrant place for all walks of local life. The best time to visit is late afternoon on Wednesday for the **St Pauli Nachtmarkt** (night market; p118).

5. Film & TV Star

South of the Reeperbahn stands the **Davidwache police station**, star of many a German crime film and TV show (most prominently *Tatort,* the world's longest running crime series and a national obsession). Festooned with ornate ceramic tiles, the station is the base for 150 officers, whose task it is to keep order in the lurid district. Anti-establishment sentiment runs deep in St Pauli, so the neighbourhood and the station have something of a love-hate relationship.

6. Party Mile

Continue down the Reeperbahn (watch out for broken glass and other evidence of last night's antics) to reach the **Grosse Freiheit party mile** (p116). At the corner of the Reeperbahn and Grosse Freiheit, **Beatles-Platz** (p116) is an abstract sculpture tracing out the Fab Four atop a vinyl record.

7. The Beatles in Hamburg

Further along Grosse Freiheit, a series of plaques commemorate key sites from the Beatles' time in Hamburg (p116). The final plaque, next to the entrance of the **Indra Club** (p125), marks the location of the band's very first gig in Germany, on 17 August 1960.

WALKING TOUR

St Pauli by Night

St Pauli and the Reeperbahn are the epicentres of Hamburg's legendary nightlife. There's so much going on here that you need a few nights to see it all. Look past the neon lights and crowded bars to discover a fascinating history popping up in between.

START	END	LENGTH
Giovanni Rocco	Kleine Haie Grosse Fische	700m; 20 minutes

1 Pizza Joint

Start your evening in St Pauli by filling up on pizza at **Giovanni Rocco** (p123). The buzzy Italian restaurant is a pre-party favourite among students and locals. The atmosphere is lively and chaotic – a true reflection of St Pauli's neighbourhood spirit.

2 Surly Dive Bar

Fortified with pizza, have a drink at dimly lit, sticker-covered **St Pauli Eck** (p124). The popular local pub on the corner of Simon-von-Utrecht-Strasse and Hein-Hoyer-Strasse also has a jukebox – essentially, it combines all the right ingredients of the perfect *Kneipe* (dive bar). Drinks are stiff and cheap; service is surly.

3 Drag Queen's Namesake

Make your way to Grosse Freiheit, the Reeperbahn's legendary party street. Olivia Jones, Germany's most famous drag queen, owns a number of bars on the strip; at **her namesake venue** (p124) you can continue easing into the St Pauli mayhem with a few cheap drinks, *Schlager* (cheesy German pop) and maybe a drag show.

4 Beatles Haunt

Pull up a stool and order a beer at **Gretel & Alfons** (p124) just like John, Paul and George used to do. There's a plaque above the door dedicated to the Beatles' ample time drinking here during their 1960s Hamburg residency. The tiny pub hasn't changed much since then; it still rocks rustic wooden interiors and cheap beers on tap. Don't forget to settle your bar tab: the story goes that Paul McCartney once did but came back to settle up years later.

5 Dive Bar & Gym

Ready for the Reeperbahn? Descend into the madness of legendary dive bar **Zur Ritze** (p117), where the full gamut of Hamburg society turns up throughout the night. Don't miss the hidden boxing gym in the cellar. Mike Tyson, Muhammad Ali and the Klitschko brothers have all trained there.

6 Eccentric Dive Bar

Down the house speciality, a caraway shot, at **Zum Silbersack** (p124), a classic Reeperbahn spot. Beware: the place can be a vortex. You might lose hours here playing darts, feeding the jukebox and chatting to its eclectic (and often quite eccentric) patrons.

7 Fish Shack

Busy from morning till night, **Kleine Haie Grosse Fische** (p123) is a timeless Hamburg institution. The *Fischbude* (fish shack) serves *Fischbrötchen* (fish sandwiches) as well as smoked fish and meats. Grab a fish sandwich for the road, which is really the best way to enjoy one in any case.

EXPERIENCES

Shop Curios at Flohschanze
FLEA MARKET

MAP: ① P104 E1

Hosted in a 19th century slaughterhouse, **Flohschanze** *(marktkultur-hamburg.de)* is Hamburg's best Saturday flea market. Hundreds of vendors sprawl across 1200 sq metres between industrial buildings to form a stockyard nirvana for thrifting. Trinket hunters and vintage junkies are sure to delight in stalls filled with a jumble of bric-a-brac. Some stands are run by professional sellers, while others have been rented by locals hosting a mini-garage sale. Expect furniture, clothing, jewellery and more – often with a touch of St Pauli's love for the alternative and counterculture. Come early before everything's picked through; the summer crowds here are thousands strong.

Get Lost in Olivia's Bermuda Triangle
NIGHTLIFE JUNCTION

Approximately 350m off the Reeperbahn's main drag, the parallel pub strip of **Grosse Freiheit** (MAP: ② P104 B1) hosts some of the district's rowdiest spots.

Germany's most famous drag queen, longtime Hamburger Olivia Jones, has built a mini empire of venues within a 50m radius of each other. These she playfully dubs her 'Bermuda Triangle'. Stumble between the original **Olivia Jones Bar** (p124; *olivia-jones.de*) and the somewhat hidden courtyard beer garden Olivias Kiez Oase (p124).

Be tickled pink by feathers and sequins galore at **Bunny Burlesque** (MAP: ③ P104 A2; €15). Weekend shows are very popular; come early for a good seat ahead of the 11.30pm start. Dip into 'porno karaoke' on Friday and Saturday nights at **Olivias Krawallschachtel** (MAP: ④ P104 A2); there's no singing, only dubbing over retro adult German film clips. Campy storylines are the funniest part. **Olivias Wilde Jungs** (MAP: ⑤ P104 B3; Olivia's Wild Boys; *Fri/Sat €5/10*) is Germany's first all-male strip club catering exclusively to women – there's a revolving door of bachelorette parties.

Walk Through German Beatlemania
MUSICAL HISTORY

Long before they forged rock 'n' roll history, the Beatles paid their dues performing in Reeperbahn pubs. On the famous Grosse Freiheit party mile, the band set the stage for their meteoric rise. At the corner of the Reeperbahn and Grosse Freiheit, stand atop the vinyl-record-shaped **Beatles-Platz** (MAP: ⑥ P104 B6) next to abstract steel sculptures of the Fab Four (including a hybrid of Ringo Starr and the band's original drummer during the Hamburg days, Pete Best).

The band's name is featured (along with those of other artists from Mos Def to Kylie Minogue) outside the Kaiserkeller (p125). A small plaque outside the Indra Club (p125) commemorates the Beatles' inaugural German gig. Another plaque at Gretel & Alfons (p124) dubs this particular pub the boys' favourite haunt.

Descend into the Reeperbahn's Fight Club HISTORIC BOXING GYM

The notorious entrance to **Zur Ritze** (MAP: 10 P104 C6; *zurritze.com*), a Reeperbahn classic *Kneipe*, is unmissable thanks to a pair of spread-eagled, high-heeled legs (belonging to the Ritze 'receptionist') painted over the door. Pass through the long laneway and you've found one of the Reeperbahn's most serious drinking dens. It even draws a few local celebrities. Down in the basement is a still-active **boxing gym** *(adult €3)*, with a fight-club culture that can only be described as heavyweight. Established in 1974 by former East German middleweight boxer Hanne Kleine, the 'boxing cellar' was historically a training hub for local street fighters and bouncers.

Relax in the 'Bosom' of St Pauli PUBLIC SQUARE

There always seems to be something going on at **Spielbudenplatz** (MAP: 11 P104 D6; *spielbudenplatz.eu*). Located in the heart of the neighbourhood, this offbeat square is where the Reeperbahn red-light district tends to transition into a vibrant place for local life. Late afternoon on Wednesday is the best time to visit, when the lively **St Pauli Nachtmarkt** (MAP: 12 P104 D6) sets up with food

ENJOY BEAUTIFUL LIVE-MUSIC VENUES

Knust
MAP: 7 P104 E1
In addition to excellent music gigs and experimental DJ sets, this sprawling former slaughterhouse hosts anything from acoustic raves to spoken-word performances. *knusthamburg.de*

Docks Prinzenbar
MAP: 8 P104 D6
With its cheeky cherubs, stucco flourishes and sparkling chandeliers, this intimate Baroque club – a former cinema – hosts stylish electro parties, concerts and queer bashes. @docksprinzenbar

Gruenspan
MAP: 9 P104 B1
Established in 1889 as a dance hall, brick-and-stucco Gruenspan became one of Germany's first discotheques and now hosts rock concerts. Industrial 2nd-floor rafters provide the perfect stage perspective. *gruenspan.de*

stalls and live bands (usually from around 6pm or 7pm). Seek out a comfy chair and knock back an Astra, Hamburg's cult beer.

In mid-May and early September, food trucks roll into the square and stick around for four or five days for the **St Pauli Food Truck Festival**.

From mid-November to Christmas, Spielbudenplatz hosts a Reeperbahn-appropriate **Christmas Market** (MAP: 13 P104 D6). If you're on the 'naughty list', shop at stands selling XXX-rated toys while sipping mulled wine. There are also strip shows, 'porno karaoke' and more 'Bad Santa'–approved fun.

Ascend a Posh St Pauli Tower   CLASSY GASTRONOMY

Watching over the eastern gateway to St Pauli since 2011, the **Tanzende Türme** (MAP: 14 P104 E6; Dancing Towers) are a Reeperbahn icon. They buck and weave by up to 3m from the vertical, resembling a dancing couple. A legendary dance hall once stood here, and the towers provide an elegant contrast to the area's general sleaze. The rooftop hosts two of the Reeperbahn's classiest addresses: prestigious steak restaurant **Clouds** (MAP: 15 P104 E6; *clouds-hamburg.de*) and the adjoining Clouds Bar (p124). In the basement you'll find Hamburg's legendary jazz lair the Mojo Club (p120).

Cheer on FC St Pauli at Its Home Stadium   FOOTBALL STADIUM

FC St Pauli has a cult following in Hamburg – you'll see its skull-and-crossbones logo on black T-shirts. The second-tier Bundesliga (Germany's pro football league) team plays at home at St Pauli's **Millerntor-Stadion** (MAP: 16 P104 E3; *fcstpauli.com/millerntor*).

The most exciting games are the 'Hamburg derbys' between FC St Pauli and Hamburger SV (HSV), the city's other major football club. These showdowns are about more than a love of the game; while HSV is associated with mainstream

---

GERMANY'S DIVE BARS

In St Pauli, *Kneipen* (dive pubs) are deeply tied to the harbour district's working-class, maritime culture. Once late-night watering holes where port workers could unwind, today they're emblematic of the district's countercultural identity. What makes a good *Kneipe*? Rustic interiors, low lights, trashy toilets. Usually there's a jukebox, pool table or dartboard. Often, smoking indoors is allowed, but paying by card isn't. Rough edges aside, *Kneipen* can make for truly warm, cosy evenings. Drinks are cheap and stiff; quirky regulars add charm. After all the other establishments have closed, trust your local *Kneipe* to stay open till sunrise.

football culture, FC St Pauli (the Bundesliga's black sheep) counters with a punk, anti-establishment identity.

Daily guided **stadium tours** *(adult/child €17.50/free)* cover the pitch and locker rooms and provide historical insights. Museum (see below) admission is included. Merch is available at the on-site fan **shop**; the skull-and-bones logo is on everything, including LGBTIQ+ rainbow flags. The shop is open Wednesday to Friday.

Uncover Football History at the FC St Pauli-Museum   CLUB MUSEUM

MAP: 17 P104 E3

Opened in 2012, the **FC St Pauli-Museum** *(fcstpauli-museum.de; adult/child €7/4)* celebrates the history and culture of an unconventional football club. The museum is run by fans and volunteers, which reflects the club's strong sense of community. Exhibits highlight the team's transformation from a local, district-level outfit (established in 1910) to a nationally competitive club. Important to this journey was the identity of St Pauli's fans as an opposing force to mainstream football culture.

Listen to Genuine Jazz at Mojo Club   JAZZ INSTITUTION

MAP: 18 P104 E6

Slink into the basement of the Tanzende Türme (p118) for a night at Hamburg's legendary jazz den

BEST ST PAULI FESTIVALS

Hamburger Kabarett-Festival
Based at St Pauli Theater, this cabaret festival has been running for more than three decades. The nightly programme lasts for nearly a month from April to May. *st-pauli-theater.de*

Schlagermove
In mid-July St Pauli hosts this extravagant street parade where everyone dresses up in 1970s fashion to celebrate German language disco songs. The procession takes place across the neighbourhood from the port area to the Reeperbahn, and the party spills over into the bars and nightclubs. *schlagermove.de*

Reeperbahn Festival
This happening live-music celebration in September covers every musical genre imaginable and fills St Pauli's venues (from seedy nightclubs to churches) with crowds and quality performances. In 2018 some events were even held in the newly minted Elbphilharmonie. Download the festival app to help make sense of it all. *reeperbahnfestival.com*

the **Mojo Club** *(mojo.de),* which hosts a stellar lineup of local and international acts. Great atmosphere, great acoustics, a discerning jazz crowd, a long cocktail menu – it's one of the city's best nights out. Sometimes there's no extra cover charge. Most acts start around 8pm. After 10pm, DJs take over the sound system.

Join the Mosh Pit at Molotow
INDIE ROCK INSTITUTION

MAP: **19** P104 **B5**

The legendary indie-rock club **Molotow** has a 30-year reputation as a 'springboard stage'. The White Stripes, Mumford & Sons, the Killers and the Black Keys are among the bands who have played in the packed, sweaty basement before reaching international acclaim.

On the right night, raw talent and St Pauli's punk crowd can come together for a truly electrifying concert experience.

Molotow is so beloved that when the venue's rental contract was terminated in 2023, Hamburgers went berserk. A demonstration under the slogan 'Molotow must stay' drew thousands of head-banging supporters, including several well-known German artists, to the club's former doorstep.

In March 2025 Molotow moved to a new location just a few steps up the Reeperbahn: the former Top Ten Club where the Beatles once rocked the stage. The rental agreement is locked in until 2037.

Boogie on StrandPauli Sands
BEACH BAR

MAP: **20** P104 **C8**

A beach bar on the Elbe River overlooking rusty shipping containers might sound like the epitome of German kitsch, but the perpetually crowded sands at **StrandPauli** *(strandpauli.de)* prove the concept works, scenic views be damned.

On a stretch of sand built over the water, the bar leans fully into campy delight with multicoloured sunloungers, traditional German breakfasts served on the weekends and *currywurst* hot off the grill.

PIRATE DISTRICT

St Pauli's nickname, the Pirate District, reflects both its working-class origins and today's counterculture scene. Originally lying outside Hamburg's city walls, port-adjacent St Pauli was a maritime workers' haven for nightlife and entertainment. Sailors' taverns, brothels and gambling joints preceded red-light Reeperbahn. Punk culture swanned into St Pauli in the late 1970s and the area began attracting activists, students and artists who turned abandoned maritime buildings into squats. Among the port city's historic wealth and prestige, St Pauli's existence is hugely symbolic. The neighbourhood proves that protest, creativity and anti-capitalism also find refuge in Hamburg.

You could say the dock's shabby scenery even adds to StrandPauli's laid-back, breezy atmosphere. In summer there's no better place to relax and catch a few rays. There are also beach yoga classes and DJ dance parties.

Get Your Beat on Aboard Frau Hedi
DANCE CAFE

MAP: 21 P104 D8

It doesn't get more kitschy than *über Deutsch* (exceptionally German) **Frau Hedi** *(frauhedi.de)*. On a boat moored permanently at Pier 10, a former sightseeing vessel now hosts a popular *Tanzkaffee* (dance cafe) Wednesday to Saturday. A jam-packed schedule of DJs dish up themed musical nights – everything from classic disco to Afrobeats to Motown soul. Check the website for dates.

GERMANY'S CBGB
The **Star Club memorial** (MAP: 22 P104 A2) honours an iconic venue that had an outsized impact despite its short, seven-year lifespan. In the 1960s the Star Club hosted legendary performances by the likes of the Beatles, Jimi Hendrix, the Bee Gees and Fats Domino. It revolted against the censorship of sanitised, Germanised versions of American rock, and its memory endures as an anti-authority haven during the Cold War era. In its heyday the Star Club welcomed nearly a million visitors annually. It closed in 1969, and the vacant building was demolished in 1987 after a fire.

Indulge in Fried Herring at Fischerhaus
SEAFOOD RESTAURANT

MAP: 23 P104 A8

Arguably the pick of the sit-down restaurants in the Fischmarkt (p106), the **Fischerhaus** *(restaurant-fischerhaus.de)* has a couple of options for an atmospheric dinner. The views are better from the upper Hafenblick (harbour views) room, but it's more casual and kid-friendly at the ground-floor Restaurant Rustikal (the 1898-built historic *Gaststube* or tavern). Prices tend to be slightly lower at Rustikal. Fried fish with *Kartoffelsalat* (potato salad) or *Bratkartoffeln* (pan-fried potatoes) is a speciality, but you could pick any seafood-and-side combo and leave satisfied.

Rappel (or Relax) on the Cap San Diego
HISTORIC FREIGHTER

MAP: 24 P104 F8

The permanently docked **Cap San Diego** *(capsandiego.de; adult/student €12/10.20)* is a decommissioned cargo freighter that's now a floating museum, hotel and high-ropes course all in one.

Roam around the beautiful 1961-built, 10,000-tonne vessel and discover its fascinating history on a self-guided tour with audioguide. Nicknamed the White Swan of the South Atlantic, the MS *Cap San Diego* transported goods to Germany from 1961 to 1982. It was under threat of being scrapped when the city of Hamburg purchased it and a team of volunteers, including former dock workers, undertook its restoration.

Eight passenger cabins have been turned into **hotel** rooms for overnight stays (a novel but rather cramped experience). A high-ropes climbing course runs across the ship's bridges and beams. Safety lines and harnesses ensure you stay out of the Elbe River.

Enjoy Paulianers' Favourite Park   WATERFRONT PARK

Hamburg's maritime tableau spreads out before 4000-sq-metre **Park Fiction** (MAP: 25 P104 B8; *park-fiction.net*). Quirky features such as plastic palm trees and a lawn in the shape of a flying carpet reflect the Paulianers (St Pauli residents) who helped create this waterfront green space.

In the early 1990s locals fearing gentrification pushed back on city plans for housing projects here. Artists, activists and neighbours came together and proposed an alternative solution: a community-designed public park inspired by art. Every playful, unusual feature of Park Fiction is the result of an idea contributed at resident meetings and workshops.

 FC ST PAULI'S JOLLY ROGER

Everywhere you turn in St Pauli you'll see residents wearing FC St Pauli's skull-and-crossbones logo. The Jolly Roger has become an unofficial symbol of St Pauli itself and not just its football team. Since the 1980s the team's fans have embraced an identity of rejecting violence and hooliganism – persistent problems in German football culture. A new wave of Pirate District fans (p120) – St Pauli residents from punks to students – has transformed the club's image with strong values opposing discrimination in all forms. In recent years the traditional black flag has even been exchanged for a rainbow LGBTIQ+ one bearing the skull-and-crossbones logo.

LISTINGS

Best Places for...

€ Budget €€ Midrange €€€ Top End

Eating

Budget Bites

Brücke 10 €
 D8

There are a gazillion fish sandwich vendors in Hamburg, but this contemporary outpost makes one of the best. Lovely tables outside. *10am-10pm*

Rindermarkthalle €
27 E2

Plentiful food stands serve everything from Mexican to Vietnamese in a market-style food court. *8am-9pm Mon-Sat*

Bakeries

Buttercrumbs Bakery €
28 D7

Gourmet Buttercrumbs doles out some of Hamburg's best *Franzbrötchen* – a must-try local favourite somewhere between a cinnamon roll and a croissant. *8am-4pm Mon-Fri, to 2pm Sat & Sun*

Café Mimosa €
29 D4

The go-to place for warm brioches, some of the yummiest cakes in town and daily-changing lunch specials. *10am-7pm Tue-Sun*

Konditorei Holger Rönnfeld €
30 D4

Sweet offerings abound at this aromatic traditional bakery. Try a *Nussecken*, a crunchy, nutty triangular pastry. *6.30am-6pm Mon-Fri, to 4pm Sat*

Late-Night Grub

Kleine Haie Grosse Fische €
 C6

St Pauli's version of the late-night kebab stop is this timeless place serving fish sandwiches as well as smoked fish and meats. *6pm-midnight Wed & Thu, 2pm-4am Fri & Sat*

Kleine Pause €
 C3

Here old-school German fast-food joint meets *Kneipe* (dive bar). It's stiff drinks and fried everything, with fittingly gruff service. *8am-3am Mon-Thu, to 5am Fri & Sat, 9am-2am Sun*

Cosy Restaurants

Giovanni Rocco €€
33 C3

Pauli's hottest pizza joint. Arrive early on weekend evenings for a table amid its bumping, pre-party atmosphere. *3pm-midnight Sun-Thu, to 1am Fri & Sat*

Clouds €€€
see **15** E6

On the 23rd floor of the **Tanzende Türme** (p118), this elegant space serves up steak and marvellous city views. Smart casual dress essential. *11.30am-2pm & 5-11pm Mon-Fri, 5-11pm Sat & Sun*

Nil €€€
 D2

Hip tri-level Nil serves a slow-food menu steered by the seasons and regional suppliers. Flavour pairings can be adventurous. The summer garden tables are dreamy. *6-10.30pm Wed-Sun*

See p104 for map of locations

Drinking

Dive Bars

Golden Pudel Club
 B8

Tiny bar-club Golden Pudel occupies a 19th-century bootleggers' jail and has ties to the German punk scene. Programming prizes underground bands and vinyl DJs. *10pm-6am*

Zum Silbersack
 C6

A diverse crowd and cheap drinks make for weird and wild evenings. Be sure to down an infamous caraway shot. *5pm-2am Mon-Thu, to 3am Fri & Sat, to 1am Sun*

St Pauli Eck
 C5

A quintessential *Kneipe*, St Pauli Eck has a jukebox, stiff pours and grumpy bar staff. Misbehaving tourists aren't welcome. *5pm-late Mon-Sat*

Gretel & Alfons
 A3

This tiny late-night cafe-bar is little changed from when the Beatles unwound here after shows. Pull up a chair at the rustic bar. Come early before it gets too packed. *6pm-6am*

Cafes

Cafe Geyer
 B7

Whether you're seeking out a house-made croissant or to nurse a wine or coffee, Cafe Geyer is a cosy place for a beverage in St Pauli. During spring, blossoming trees beautify the outdoor seating. *10am-1am*

Constant Grind
 F2

Located halfway up to the Hamburg Bunker's rooftop garden, Constant Grind cafe is an excellent hangout. Floor-to-ceiling windows offer impeccable skyline views. *9am-6pm*

Cocktail Bars

Clockers
 B4

This whimsical, forest-inspired cocktail den has garnered many mixology awards. Sip seriously imaginative concoctions amid mossy walls, branches and fairy lights. *8pm-1am Wed & Thu, to 3am Fri & Sat*

Clouds Bar
 E6

The elegant bar above Clouds (p118) is popular with an upmarket crowd, who come here for the highballs and perfectly mixed cocktails. When the weather's clear, head to the lounge chairs at the open-air Heaven's Nest right at the summit. There's a 'casual elegant' dress code. *11.30am-late Mon-Fri, from noon Sat & Sun*

Tower Bar
43 E7

Drop by this 14th-floor lounge at the Hotel Hafen for a low-key evening with a slightly classier vibe (in comparison to the Reeperbahn, at least). Harbour views will keep you entranced. *6pm-2am*

LGBTIQ+ Spots

Olivia Jones Bar
44 A2

The Grosse Freiheit bar that started Olivia Jones' party empire. Look forward to *Schlager* (cheesy German pop) on stereo and drag performances. Rumour has it that Russian president Putin has been a guest here. *8pm-1am Sun-Thu, to 2am Fri, to 3am Sat*

Olivias Kiez Oase
45 A3

Find 'Olivia's Neighbourhood Oasis' tucked away in a Grosse Freiheit courtyard with beer garden vibes. It's the perfect escape when the party strip's rowdiness becomes too much. *8.30pm-1am Fri, 7.30pm-2am Sat*

WunderBar
46 C5

An extravagant gay bar with luminous red interiors, WunderBar has been around since the 1990s and shows no signs of slowing down. Up-for-a-good-time DJs spin everything from *Schlager* to electro. *10pm-late*

DJ & Live Music Bars

Indra Club
47 B1

Live rock and indie acts keep up an enduring legacy at the Indra. The interior is vastly different from when the Beatles played here in the 1960s, though. There's a fine beer garden. *hours vary*

Kaiserkeller
48 B2

On the Grosse Freiheit party strip, this live-music venue has a storied history of big names from Kylie Minogue to Mos Def (the Beatles also played here often). These days, open-mic nights and jam sessions keep an underground vibe. *hours vary*

Komet
49 C7

Vinyl and vinyl only spins at this treasure of a music bar. Nightly themes range from ska and rocksteady to '60s garage punk and hip-hop. Order a Helga (a sweetish house drink), which will have everything sounding dreamy in no time. *9pm-late*

Lunacy
50 C5

This lively bar oozes St Pauli attitude – the music stays pretty intense, with DJs spinning punk, ska, rock and metal, and even the table football is played seriously in these parts. *9pm-4am Sun-Thu, to dawn Fri & Sat*

Shopping

St Pauli Attire

Crazy Jeans
51 C6

Black is everything here, with leather studs and all manner of pirate motifs filling this St Pauli classic. A few brand names turn up from time to time, but it's mostly about taking a slightly angry, sideways glance at life. *noon-10pm*

Loonies
52 C6

Stop in for clothing and accessories emblazoned with the St Pauli logo and plenty of retro fashion choices. *noon-9pm Sun-Thu, to 10pm Fri & Sat*

Flohschanze
see **1** E1

At Hamburg's best flea market hundreds of vendors set up outdoors in the hip Karolinenviertel. Find your St Pauli style here. *8am-4pm Sat*

Vinyl Records

Zardoz Records
53 E1

With a little something for everyone, Zardoz has lovely staff, and new and secondhand vinyl and CDs. *noon-6pm Mon-Fri, from 11am Sat*

Groove City
54 F1

Discover surprising finds across well-curated, genre-spanning stock – hip-hop to Latin rhythms and jazz. *noon-7pm Mon-Fri, from 11am Sat*

Otaku Records
55 B4

A DJ or club-goer's best friend, Otaku has all electronic styles from techno to UK garage. Do some backroom diving – Hardy, the owner, has recommendations. *2-7.30pm Mon-Fri, 1-6.30pm Sat*

Explore
Altona & the Elbmeile

One of the coolest corners of Hamburg, Altona is a window on local life just a short S-Bahn ride from the city centre. Formerly its own small city, the area boasts waterfront restaurants and *Kieze* (neighbourhood communities) such as Schanzenviertel and Karoviertel that beat to the modern rhythms of its countercultural scene.

Down the hill, near the water, you can explore the Elbmeile, a string of tempting restaurants and eclectic boutiques. Make time to wander aimlessly off the Elbmeile and into Altona proper; it's only in this way that you'll get a taste of the neighbourhood's character and charm.

Getting Around

Walking and cycling
Your feet will get you around Altona just fine, but cycling will certainly make exploration a lot easier, especially if you want to visit other neighbourhoods. The St Pauli Piers has designated bike parking.

S-Bahn
The S-Bahn connects Hamburg-Altona station to Hamburg Hauptbahnhof in only 5 minutes; services run every few minutes throughout the day.

Regional trains
Many Hamburg trains, including long-distance services, begin or end at Hamburg-Altona.

Dockland office complex (p131)
PHOTO-SELECT/SHUTTERSTOCK

THE BEST

RIVERSIDE PROMENADE
Elbmeile (p130)

SCENIC VIEWPOINT
Altonaer Balkon (p136)

CULTURAL SPACE
Fabrik (p139)

MODERN ARCHITECTURE
Dockland (p131)

CULTURAL CENTRE
Rote Flora (p136)

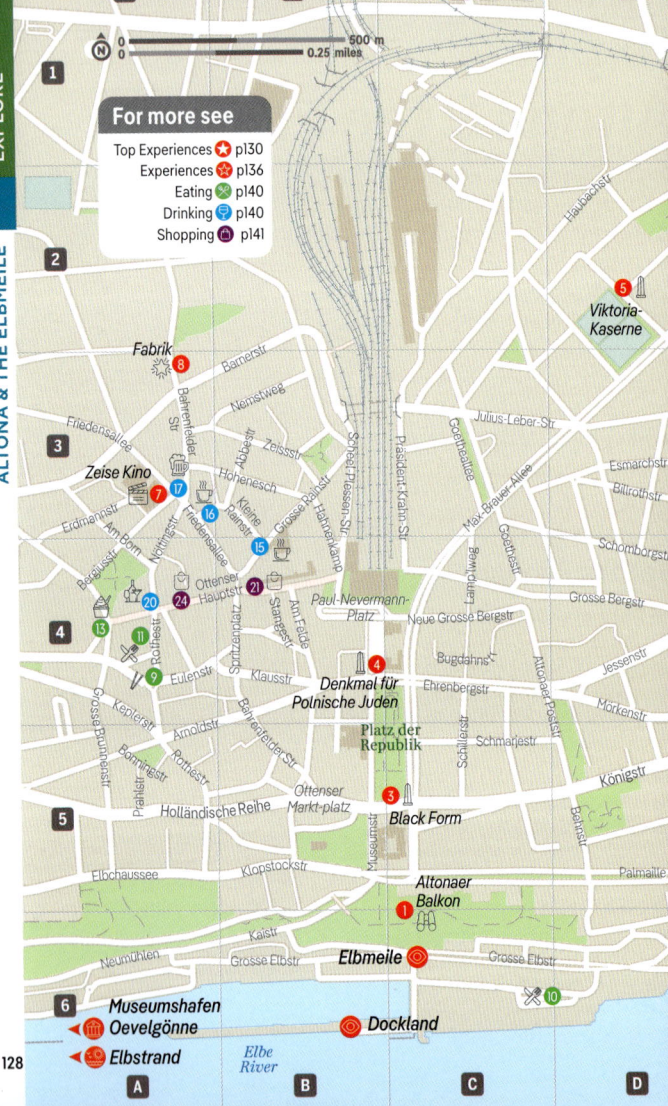

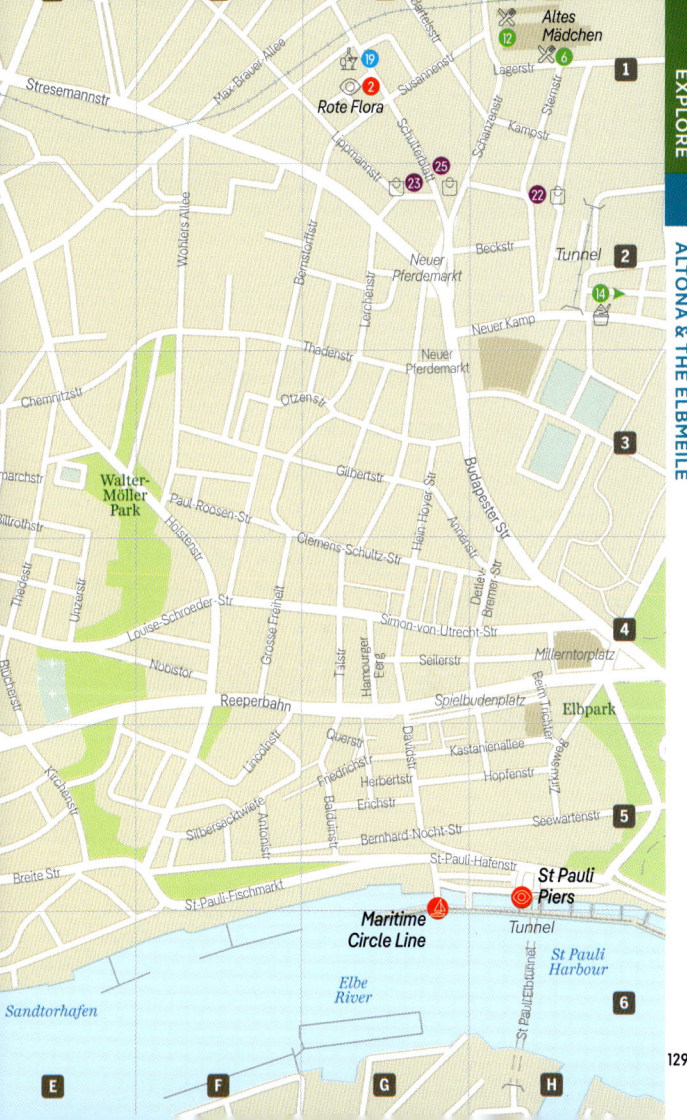

★ **TOP EXPERIENCE**

Elbmeile

Hamburg's prime riverside real estate, the **Elbmeile** (Elbe Mile) promenade is studded with beach cafes and waterfront bars ranging from lively to laid-back. The joy of strolling here isn't about any one attraction but instead about harbourside views and following wherever the fresh breeze takes you.

MAP P128 **C6**

PLANNING TIP
Cycle the 4km along the Elbmeile from the Museumshafen Oevelgönne to the St Pauli Piers, or take the ferry from Museumshafen Oevelgönne to the Fischmarkt (p106) and then walk to St Pauli Piers (about 1km).

Museumshafen Oevelgönne

At the furthest western edge of the Elbmeile, the **Museumshafen Oevelgönne** (MAP P128 **A6**; Museum Harbour Oevelgönne) is a bastion of maritime nostalgia. Here a dockside exhibition of restored sailing ships and working boats from the 19th and 20th centuries harks back to the former fishing village of Oevelgönne. If you're looking for off-the-beaten-track treasures, Oevelgönne is it. Its **Elbstrand** (MAP P128 **A6**) is a hot spot for sun-lounging and a rare sandy place where barbecuing is allowed. There's also a beach club, elegant architecture by David Chipperfield and plenty of harbour sights including a section of historic captain's cottages.

St Pauli Piers

The Elbmeile continues eastwards along the riverfront to the Fischmarkt (p106) and geographically ends at what's known as the **St Pauli Piers** (MAP P128 **H5**; sometimes also called by its proper name, Landungsbrücken). Welcome to Hamburg's central harbour. Ten pontoons dating back to 1907 berth under elegant rooftops offering prime architectural examples of *Jugendstil* (p74; Germany's late-19th-century Art Nouveau movement). The central terminal building and its adjoining

St Pauli Piers
SHEVIAKOVA KATERYNA/SHUTTERSTOCK

clock tower are often a crowded chaos of cruise passenger groups and cruise staff loudly hawking last-minute spots on their tours. Continuing down the waterfront, you'll soon reach Speicherstadt and the Elbphilharmonie (about a 20-minute walk; p89).

Dockland

Just past the Fischmarkt the Elbe riverside goes from historic to modern, seemingly in a matter of steps. The change happens at the **Dockland office complex** (MAP P128 **B6**), a sublime example of modern maritime architecture. From the promenade the striking waterfront structure appears to jut right from the water (it's actually poised on a small, artificial stretch carving into the Elbe River). Finished in 2006, Dockland has a sleek design that resembles a stepped ship. Though

Scan this QR code for a riverside Oevelgönne self-guided tour.

ELBMEILE MISNOMER

The name Elbmeile ('Elbe Mile') is misleading: the riverfront isn't 1 mile long but 2.5 miles (4km). The walk isn't all promenade either; cruising along on a bike is much better.

the building is for private use only, you can go up to its 'bow', a rooftop terrace accessed by a public stairwell (there's no lift). From here there's a prime, lesser-known vantage point on the river from where you can gaze at cruise ships and other river traffic.

Harbour Cruises

Most harbour cruises depart from the St Pauli Piers. Board a traditional *Barkassen* (petite, historic passenger boat) for one- to two-hour tours. There are a range of operators; decide by the kind of cruise you're interested in (options include sunset scenery, history and heading off the river to explore Hamburg's canals). Evening harbour tours are the most popular because you

Övelgönne
LAPA SMILE/SHUTTERSTOCK

can enjoy the sight of the illuminated warehouses; these tours should be booked ahead. If you're looking to see harbourside sights without too much time pressure, the **Maritime Circle Line** (MAP P128 G5) offers hop-on, hop-off vessels stopping at all the main attractions, including the Internationales Maritimes Museum (p87).

Local Ferries

The Elbmeile promenade might be made for walking, but consider taking in at least part of it with one of **HADAG's commuter ferries**. Docking at the Museumshafen Oevelgönne as well as the Fischmarkt, St Pauli Piers and the Elbphilharmonie, these small vessels shuttle residents along the river but can be just as good for a water-based sightseeing tour. The experience is authentically local and a more tranquil way of exploring than an official harbour cruise. The St Pauli Piers is the key hub for HADAG's seven commuter lines, which criss-cross the Elbe River. Line 62 will take you on the 30-minute journey along the river from Museumshafen Oevelgönne to the Elbphilharmonie; ferries run roughly every 15 minutes throughout the day.

Historic Harbour Village

Övelgönne's origins date back to the 17th century, when it emerged as a small fishing and boatbuilding village. By the 19th century industrialisation and harbour expansion had seen many traditional wooden houses fall into disrepair as locals moved inland. Övelgönne was gradually incorporated into Hamburg during the 20th century. It wasn't until the 1970s that preservation initiatives began bringing the harbour's historic charm back to life.

STAYING IN ALTONA

Save a few euros by staying in Altona, just off the Elbmeile and abounding in casual eateries, homey pubs and budget lodgings. The village-like area around the station has plentiful well-priced restaurants open late. Residential vibes by day and crowd-free evening streets make for an attractive change from central Hamburg, which can be reached in just 20 minutes by frequent trains and buses.

WALKING TOUR

Ottensen: Hamburg's Quiet Achiever

West of Hamburg-Altona Station, Ottensen is where many visitors fall in love with Hamburg. There are few traditional attractions here, but you'll feel as though you've stumbled into a part of the city where people go about their authentic daily life. Neither showy nor extravagant, Ottensen could be Hamburg's coolest corner.

START	END	LENGTH
Klippkroog	Familien-Eck	900m; 20 minutes

1 Local Favourite

Ask any Altona local about **Klippkroog** and you'll probably hear nothing but praise. The crowd favourite cafe serves dishes with a focus on seasonal regional produce – expect northern German classics with an inventive twist. A cosy interior with wooden tables, lots of natural light and good coffee come together here for a perfect start to the day.

2 WWII Memorial

Walk through the leafy surrounds of the public square Paul-Nevermann-Platz and you'll reach a solemn granite monument, the **Denkmal für Polnische Juden** (p137). The landmark commemorates the forced deportation of over 800 Polish Jews from Altona on 28 October 1938 during the *Polenaktion* (Polish Action).

3 Local Museum

Continuing south, leafy green space turns into a different public square, Platz der Republik. Follow Museumsstrasse to the **Altonaer Museum**, where you can take a quick whirl through northern German arts and cultural history. Highlights include farmhouse parlours and a hall of farmhouse models; there's also a *Wunderkammer* (cabinet of curiosities) for little ones to dig through.

4 Danish Homewares

The Altona outpost of designer (yet affordable) Danish homewares shop **Søstrene Grene** (p141) is a neighbourhood favourite. Here you'll find an array of simple, stylish items that capture the essence of Scandinavian design. Collections featuring nautical colours and coastal motifs appeal to Hamburg's maritime roots – and of course there are lots of commonalities between the city and Denmark through historical trading around the North Sea.

5 Coffee & Cake

Even if you miss the morning at cheery **Café Mikkels** (p140), which mixes affability with pastel style, grab a seat outside and catch the afternoon sun. The delightful German tradition of *Kaffee und Kuchen* (coffee and cake) is perfection here. The cake menu changes often, and every one is whipped up in-house.

6 Classic Dive Bar

It may be a simple hole in the wall, but **Familien-Eck** (p141) is everything a good German *Eckkneipe* (corner dive bar) should be. Friendly, unassuming service shows that, even though it's now integrated into Hamburg proper, Altona is still a village at heart. Hobnob with locals; on weekends, DJs spin in the city's tiniest DJ booth.

EXPERIENCES

Relax with Views on Altona's 'Balcony' PANORAMIC PARK

In Altona you can watch the comings and goings on Hamburg's river and port from one of the best vantage points in the city. The appropriately named **Altonaer Balkon** (MAP: ❶ P128 **C6**; Altona Balcony) offers some wonderful harbour views from its panoramic heights.

The park's name is not at all hyperbolic; it sits on a hilltop elevated 27m above the Elbe River, offering sweeping vistas of the hustle and skyline – see if you can pick out some of the notable buildings, such as the Elbphilharmonie (p89). The balcony's highest point, its main lookout terrace, is worth the ascent, but great views are abundant throughout the park. Come for a picnic or a stroll along the pretty paths. The latter is best timed for when the sun is going down.

Catch a Cultural Event at Rote Flora ANTI-GENTRIFICATION LANDMARK

MAP: ❷ P128 **G1**

One of the most outstanding remnants of the steadily gentrifying Altona area's rougher days is the graffiti-covered **Rote Flora** *(rote-flora.de; free)*. From the outside the once dapper 19th-century theatre building now looks one step away from demolition, but it's one of the gritty, anti-establishment Schanzenviertel's most important activism landmarks.

In 1989, after plans emerged to redevelop the Flore Theatre into a commercial venue, activists occupied it; in 2014 the Hamburg government granted a legal protection prohibiting business development of the site. Rote Flora remains under the control of activists and is now a *autonomes Zentrum* (autonomous centre) run by politically oriented groups. Though from the outside Rote Flora appears unkempt (it's a popular base for those who are sleeping rough), it remains an active alternative cultural centre and a firm reminder to developers that gentrification is to be taken seriously in an area in flux. Check the website to see its busy calendar of performances, literary readings and protests.

Pay Your Respects at a Holocaust Memorial PUBLIC ART

In front of the Altona Rathaus (town hall) sits an ominous-looking black cuboid structure. Its colour and shape contrast strikingly against the white-lacquered, neo-Renaissance town hall, once a grand train station. The cube is an abstract art installation and memorial by Jewish-American conceptual and minimal artist Sol LeWitt entitled ***Black Form*** (MAP: ❸ P128 **C5**). Featureless and imposing, the sculpture is made of reinforced concrete coated in black paint. *Black Form* is dedicated to the Jews of Altona (p139) who were expelled and eventually murdered during the Holocaust.

Visit a Memorial to Altona's Polish Jews   HOLOCAUST MEMORIAL

Nestled within the greenery of Paul-Nevermann-Platz, a short walk from Hamburg-Altona Station, a granite monument commemorates Holocaust victims. The **Denkmal für Polnische Juden** (MAP: ④ P128 B4) remembers the forced deportation of over 800 Polish Jews from Altona during the Germany-spanning *Polenaktion* (Polish Action) on 28 October 1938.

On that day more than 800 Polish nationals in Altona were arrested, detained at the nearby Viktoria Barracks and then deported to Poland. Across Germany the *Polenaktion* forcibly expelled over 17,000 Polish Jews.

Walk Through the Sombre Viktoria Barracks   HOLOCAUST HISTORY

The former **Viktoria-Kaserne** (MAP: ⑤ P128 D2; *gedenkstaetten-in-hamburg.de; free*) is where hundreds of Polish Jews were forcibly brought on 28 October 1938 as part of the *Polenaktion*. The next stop was Altona train station, from where they were deported to Poland without housing, food or documentation, creating a humanitarian crisis.

Today the barracks is a memorial site and exhibition space managed by the non-profit Foundation of Hamburg Memorials. Entering the **denkXmal stairwell exhibition**, visitors walk through the barracks' harrowing history in the form of murals, archival photographs and informative displays. The most evocative part is the former riding and drill hall, which was the detainees' assembly point.

 A DANISH HARBOUR

Altona began as a small settlement under Danish rule. In 1640 Christian IV of Denmark established the town as a free port and trading hub in direct competition with Hamburg; its strategic location and religious tolerance helped it flourish as part of Denmark until Prussia fought for control of it and won. By the 17th and 18th centuries Altona had become a multicultural hub, home to Jewish, Dutch and other migrant communities. By the 19th century expanding urbanisation had seen Altona become integrated into Hamburg proper, while the neighbouring village of Ottensen – also historically ruled by Denmark – had become part of Altona.

A UNIQUE BEER

Every year Hamburg breweries get together to make the world's one and only Senatsbock. The ritual started in the harbour city during the 1950s but had been discontinued by the 1960s. A new group of breweries revived the tradition in 2014. Nine makers now participate in the beloved event, including several craft breweries such as Ratsherrn (at Altes Mädchen). Every January the keg-tapping ceremony – a big party of local beer enthusiasts in top hats and regional costumes – takes place. You can buy the beer and Senatsbock merch around the city until they sell out.

English translations are limited, so a translation app is key unless you book an English guided tour in advance; email *denkXmal@fux-eg.org* to make arrangements.

Savour a Craft Beer-paired Dinner Menu   TASTING EXPERIENCE

Hamburg's got a lot to get craft-beer geeks in a tizzy, with over 20 craft breweries opening across the city and forming an exciting scene. One of the most prominent is Altona-based **Ratsherrn brewery**. Tasting tours are offered at the brewery, but there's an even more interesting sampling experience just around the corner at the restaurant **Altes Mädchen** (MAP: 6 P128 H1; *altes-maedchen.com*).

On-staff beer sommeliers suggest Ratsherrn pairings guided by your tastes and Altes Mädchen's enticing menu of modern European fare. Many dishes show regional inspiration. You might try a burger made from northern German (Rügen Island) beef, a *Bratwurst* trio or crispy pork knuckle.

The building was once a 19th-century animal market, and its lofty red-brick interiors make for a complete culinary destination. Explore across an in-house bakery, a coffee roastery and a garden – or the brewpub, where you can continue working through the Altes Mädchen (Old Girl) beer cellar. It has around 30 choices on tap and 50-some in bottles.

Catch a Mystery Film at Zeise Kino   ARTHOUSE CINEMA

MAP: 7 P128 A3

Excellent local cinema **Zeise Kino** (*zeise.de*; tickets Mon-Fri/Sat & Sun €10/11) skips the mainstream releases and shows arthouse films in their original version (ie with German subtitles) on Original Tuesdays. The boutique movie theatre is a characterful experience with old industrial vibes and a mix of retro and modern decor. You even get free popcorn.

Stay later for the sneak preview at 10.30pm, when a surprise film is shown in its original language before its official German release. These tickets are sold on a first-come, first-served basis.

During the summer, Zeise Kino also hosts an open-air cinema (with films in their original language) in the gorgeous hidden courtyard of Hamburg's Rathaus (p38).

Treat Yourself to an Evening at Fabrik
PERFORMANCE VENUE

MAP: **8** P128 **A3**

Factory turned concert hall **Fabrik** *(Factory; fabrik.de)* is Altona's most iconic entertainment venue. For over 50 years the space has stayed true to its founding intention to combine arts, culture and community events for neighbourhood residents under a single roof. The building's former life as a metalworks and machinery factory makes for impressive industrial digs that add ambience to classical concerts and dance-party club nights. There's a particularly good rotation of international comedians and rock bands of bygone eras (they may no longer top the charts, but you're sure to know their big hits). The cultural lineup spans theatre, film and flea market nights; check the website for the schedule and to purchase event tickets.

 ALTONA JEWISH HISTORY

Before the Holocaust, Altona was home to one of the largest Jewish populations in northern Germany. A lack of religious freedom in pre-Reformation Hamburg saw Altona, which was under Danish sovereignty, become a safe haven for Ashkenazi Jews, Sephardi Jews and other minorities. In 1660 the city granted Jews formal royal protection letters that ensured their safety to settle and practise their religion here. This attracted families fleeing persecution across Europe. Altona became a centre for scholarship and home to the Altona Chief Rabbinate (the religious authority for northern Germany). By the early 20th century, before Nazi persecution, Altona's Jewish community was estimated to number 2500.

LISTINGS

Best Places for...

€ Budget €€ Midrange €€€ Top End

See p128 for map of locations

Eating

Quick Eats

Flying Market €
9 A4
Cool Vietnamese outpost Flying Market is popular for its fresh, authentic cooking. Its pho (soup), noodle dishes and *bun* (rice-noodle salads) are among the best Asian dining in town. *11.30am-10.30pm*

Atlantik Fisch €€
10 C6
At this simple cafe run by one of Hamburg's top seafood vendors you can sample 20 varieties of *Fischbrötchen* (fish sandwiches). *6am-4pm Mon-Fri, from 7am Sat*

Tide €€
11 A4
Part cafe (sandwiches, soups, cakes and coffee) and part delicatessen (olive oils, preserves made in-house from foraged berries); unique decor includes driftwood from Danish beaches, some of which has been turned into artworks for sale. *8am-6pm Mon-Fri, from 10am Sat & Sun*

Contemporary Dining

Bullerei €€€
 12 H1
A real buzz bounces off the walls of this converted slaughter-house – don't come here for a quiet romantic dinner. Steak dishes and Italian-inflected choices are on offer in one of the city's coolest dining spaces with lovely high ceilings. *11am-11pm*

Sweet Treats

Eisliebe €
13 A4
Some of the yummiest ice cream you'll ever taste is scooped in this little hole in the wall (look for the queues). There are always a dozen handmade, all-natural flavours – definitely go for fresh berries on top. *noon-9pm*

Minus €
 14 H2
Disco, cocktails and homemade ice cream – what could be better? Enjoy an Aperol spritz (Germans' favourite summer drink) with a late-night scoop of mint brownie or salted caramel. DJ parties happen regularly; check Instagram for details. *5pm-2am Mon-Thu, to 3am Fri, 3pm-3am Sat, to 11.30pm Sun*

Drinking

Charming Cafes

Café Knuth
15 B4
Sip espresso among students and creative types at this modern, spacious two-storey cafe or grab a picnic table outside and enjoy your drinks in the open air. Lively atmosphere from morning till night. *9am-late*

Café Mikkels
16 A3
Ease into the day with all-organic eggs for breakfast or sit outside and catch the afternoon sun. The coffee? As excellent as you'd expect. *9am-6pm Mon-Sat, from 10am Sun*

Cosy Pubs

Familien-Eck
 A3

This Altona classic is everything a good neighbourhood joint should be: friendly, unassuming and laid-back. Patrons are wide-ranging, taking in everyone from older locals to students. Who doesn't love an affordable bar tab? *3pm-5am*

Zum Schellfischposten
18 D6

Located not far from the Fischmarkt (p106), Hamburg's oldest and last remaining seamen's pub exudes historic charm. The century-old institution is named after the former *Schellfischbahn* train line transporting fish from the market to Altona station. *noon-midnight Mon & Wed Sat, 10am-10pm Sun*

Cocktail Bars

Katze
19 G1

Small and sleek, this kitty (*Katze* means 'cat') has the crowd purring over well-priced cocktails and great music (there's dancing on weekends). It's one of the most popular among the watering holes on the Schanzenviertel booze strip. *1pm-3am Mon-Sat, to midnight Sun*

Reh Bar
20 A4

If you could bottle the Altona spirit and turn it into a bar, Reh Bar would be it. Cosy and welcoming, and good for a morning coffee as well as a late-night cocktail, it always draws a fun crowd. It stays open as long as it's busy. *10am-midnight Sun-Wed, to 2am Thu, to 4am Fri & Sat*

Shopping

Home Design

Søstrene Grene
21 B4

Simple yet stylish, functional and fun: the homewares on offer at the Altona location of a Danish chain reference the shared maritime history of northern Germany and neighbouring Denmark. *10am-8pm Mon-Wed & Sat, to 9pm Thu & Fri*

Wohnkultur 66
22 H2

What began as an obsession with world-renowned Danish furniture-maker Finn Juhl has turned into a love affair with Danish design in general. Many of the pieces in this charming converted warehouse are works of art. They're priced accordingly. *noon-6pm Tue-Fri, to 4pm Sat*

Designer Clothing

2nd Fit
23 G2

Serious thrifting at affordable prices; there's a lot of stock, so expect to spend time perusing. At the end you pay based on your total haul's weight in kilograms (not on individual items), so earnest digging for labels does pay off. *11am-8pm Mon-Sat*

B.Sweet
24 A4

Cute, colourful B.Sweet specialises in lingerie and handmade chocolates. Fun and whimsy abounds, from brightly coloured negligées to pralines in unique flavours such as limoncello and *crème brûlée*. *noon-6pm Tue-Fri, 11am-3pm Sat*

Vintage Revivals
25 G2

From neon-lit signs to hipster staff, this vintage shop right on Schulterblatt is all about personality. Clothing racks have been diligently sorted through; nothing is necessarily cheap per se, but it's all priced by designer and condition (which is usually quite good). *11am-8pm Mon-Sat*

Hamburg Toolkit

Family Travel	144
Accommodation	145
Food, Drink & Nightlife	146
LGBTIQ+ Travel	148
Health & Safe Travel	149
Responsible Travel	150
Accessible Travel	152
Nuts & Bolts	153
Language	154

Spielbudenplatz (p117), St Pauli
DIEGO GRANDI/SHUTTERSTOCK

Family Travel

Hamburg is an excellent city for exploring with little ones. Panoramic heights, promenade strolls and museums that entrance both parents and children are among the highlights of what families can enjoy here.

The Skinny on Strollers

The crowds and cobblestones at the **Fischmarkt** are challenging but possible with a stroller, but trams, buses and the expansive Hauptbahnhof are a nightmare to navigate with one. The **Hamburg Bunker** does not offer stroller access. At the **Elbphilharmonie**, visit the observation deck by lift, not the famously long escalator.

HIGH-SPEED TRAINS

Kids aged 14 and under ride Deutsche Bahn services for free. When booking, make sure to get them tickets too and reserve their seat (at extra cost). Even if they're riding on your lap, extra space can make life easier.

Miniatur Wunderland

If you only have time for one attraction, make it  Miniatur Wunderland (p88). Parents enjoy it as much as kids do.

Farm Adventures

A farm visit outside the city – around an hour by train or less by car – is memorable, fresh-air fun. Tour the regenerative farm **Gut Haidehof** (gut-haidehof.de) and build your own basket of produce. At the organic farm **Wilkenhoff** (wilkenshoff.de), pick orchard apples, enjoy handmade pies and cakes in the cafe and stroll the petting zoo. In winter Wilkenhoff becomes a magical little countryside Christmas market.

Kid-Friendly Dining

Meals in Hamburg are family-friendly. **Kartoffelkeller** (p52) dishes up potatoes cooked every which way. At **Laufauf** (p50) yummy casseroles are packed with (hidden) vegetables and introduce little ones to *Schnitzel* and *Spätzle* (similar to mac 'n' cheese).

Public Transport

Day tickets (€7.80) cover one adult and three children aged six to 14; kids five and under ride free.

BRENT HOFACKER/SHUTTERSTOCK

Accommodation

Hamburg has excellent hotels, and standards are generally high across all budgets; even basic accommodation will likely be clean and comfortable.

Where to Stay if You Love...

Bar-hopping & Buzzy Vibes
St Pauli (p103) is a vibrant, diverse neighbourhood with well-priced bars and restaurants. Pubs stay open to the wee hours (some never close). A short stagger home is awfully nice.

LGBTIQ+ Nightlife & Brunching
St Georg (p71) is Hamburg's LGBTIQ+ district, and queer-friendly fun abounds. On boutique shopping strip Lange Reihe you can indulge in all-day breakfasts and classic cocktails on charming pavement terraces.

Museums & History
Speicherstadt & HafenCity (p85), easy walking distance to museums, the waterfront and the historic centre, puts you close to all the sights. Hotels are nice and quiet but not budget-friendly.

Fine Dining & Culture
Neustadt (p55) flaunts Hamburg's classiest gastronomy, riverside scenery, historic theatres and the classical-music district KomponistenQuartier. Everything can be explored easily on foot.

Fewer Crowds & a Local Vibe
Altona (p127) has a wonderful neighbourhood feel and great shopping and dining. Generally quiet streets make for a good night's sleep.

OUR PICK

We Love to Stay in...

Ottensen (p134)
Tucked into the Altona district, Ottensen is where many visitors lose their heart to Hamburg. The area is less about specific attractions and more about wandering residential streets without an itinerary. Charming cafes and unpretentious pubs are neighbourhood staples, and eclectic shopping spans home design and prime vintage hunting.

HOW MUCH FOR A NIGHT IN A

Hostel dorm
from €20

Double room
from €60

Family apartment
from €200

Food, Drink & Nightlife

⚠ Allergies & Intolerances

Hamburg is highly accommodating of food intolerances. By EU regulation, restaurants must number or letter-code allergens beside every dish on their menus. A legend for the ingredients is usually on a separate page or at the bottom. Many large supermarkets are stocked with lactose-free and gluten-free options. Bio (organic) supermarket chains such as Denn's carry a wider selection of such products.

❓ HOW TO ASK...

Is this gluten free?
Ist das glutenfrei?
Does this contain nuts?
Enthält das Nüsse?
Is there a vegan option?
Gibt es eine vegane Option?

GO PLANT-BASED

In eco-conscious Hamburg, prepare to be spoiled with vegan options. The highest number of fully vegan restaurants and cafes are in St Pauli and micro-districts Schanzenviertel and Karoviertel. Baked goods and bowls abound, and there are also several *Vöner* (vegan doner) stands. Most supermarkets also have fully stocked plant-based refrigerators.

Kiosks

In Hamburg, kiosks (convenience stores) aren't just for quick stops; they're for hanging out. Outdoor tables invite you to buy a beer and linger. Viewings of big matches are popular, and some late-night stores even play loud music and erupt into dance parties. Be warned: guest toilets aren't part of the experience.

HOW TO... Ask for the Bill

'Die Rechnung, bitte'.

If you're dining with company, you might be asked if the bill is together or separate.
Service charges are usually not included on bills; tips very much reflect customer satisfaction. In restaurants, tipping 5–10% is standard; in cafes and bars, round to the nearest euro.
When paying by card, specify the total amount you wish to pay (tip included), as many payment machines don't take you through a tipping option.
When paying cash, name the total change you want back from the amount given ('Ten euros back, please'). *'Stimmt so'* means keep the change.

PRICE RANGES

The following price ranges reflect the average cost of a main course:
€ less than €12
€€ €12–22
€€€ more than €22

OPENING HOURS

Cafes
10am–6pm
Restaurants
11am–10pm
Pubs
5pm–2am or later

Going Out

Dive bars The cornerstone of Hamburg's drinking culture is a classic German *Kneipe* (dive bar). These neighbourhood pubs are known for cheap drinks and rustic interiors. Most stay open until the last customer staggers out; some are open 24 hours. Find loads around St Pauli. Some *(Raucherkneipen)* allow smoking.

Beach bars Undeterred by *Schmuddelwetter* (drizzly weather), beach bars promise a sunlounger on sand 365 days a year.

Brewery bars At these old-style beer cellars or other traditional drinking houses the beer used to be (and sometimes still is) brewed on the premises.

Craft breweries Hamburg is home to Germany's most active and experimental craft beer scene. Many are located a decent train ride from the city centre.

Nightclubs Don't even think of visiting a Hamburg nightclub before midnight; some don't get going until 2am.

FROM LEFT: FOOD IMPRESSIONS/SHUTTERSTOCK, DIETMAR RAUSCHER/SHUTTERSTOCK

HOW MUCH FOR A

Draft beer in a pub
€3–5

Craft beer
€6

Beer from a kiosk
€2

Cappuccino in a cafe
€4

Aperol spritz
€6–8

Craft cocktail
€15–18

Club entry
€25

Drag or burlesque show
€10–15

LGBTIQ+ Travellers

Hamburg is popular with *Schwule* (gay) and *Lesbische* (lesbian) travellers, with the rainbow flag flying especially proudly in St Georg.

COOLEST SOUVENIR

At the **FC St Pauli Museum shop**, pick up an iconic LGBTIQ+ rainbow flag with the team's skull-and-crossbones logo. It stands for inclusivity in football culture.

Gaybourhood

St Georg is Hamburg's de facto LGBTIQ+ neighbourhood. Along main thoroughfare the Lange Reihe, the LGBTIQ+ community's presence spans a gay funeral home and the historic **Café Gnosa**. Widely considered to be the city's first openly gay cafe, it's a favourite for LGBTIQ+ cultural events and delightful brunches.

Gay bars and clubs abound in St Georg and the nightlife here – some of Hamburg's best – is resoundingly inclusive and queer-friendly. The range of venues is wide, from kitschy and swinging **Pick Up** to grand, historic cocktail spots such as **M & V Bar**.

Don't forget to stop outside the medieval **Heilige Dreieinigkeitskirche** (p77) for a photo op with the gigantic rainbow-painted letters spelling *Liebe* ('Love') across its entrance.

HAMBURG PRIDE

St Georg street celebrations, a big parade, drag shows and much more – Hamburg Pride Week is not to be missed.

OUR PICKS

Queer Nightlife in St Pauli

CLASSIC NIGHT OUT
Olivia Jones Bar (p124) Gay-bar institution for *Schlager* (German pop music), DJs and drag performances.

SACRED SPACE
WunderBar (p125) Gay bar flaunting over-the-top decor and lighting. Extravagant or kitsch? Depends who you ask. DJs spinning *Schlager* and disco guarantee good times.

BRING THE QUIRK
Olivias Krawallschachtel (p116) 'Porno karaoke' bar whose backdrop is retro German soft-core adult films.

Resources

● *heinfiete.de* Info and cost-free testing in St Georg. ● *intervention-hamburg.de* Feminist and femme-queer centre in St Pauli. ● *blu.fm* Free print and online mag for the regional north. ● *maenner.media* Queer news and affairs. ● *l-mag.de* German-language, bimonthly lesbian magazine – print and online.

Health & Safe Travel

Hamburg is generally a safe city and most people visit without encountering any problems. Stay alert around the Reeperbahn.

Reeperbahn Survival Guide

Theft is a problem here. Keep an eye on your belongings on the street and also in bars.

In some pubs people might approach you for change or to sell you something. They move along quickly when you politely decline.

Beware a common 'free entry' scam: door staff lure in passersby with bargain shows, leaving them to discover the mandatory drink minimum (usually at least €25) too late.

Illegal Medications
Some anxiety and pain medications are considered illegal narcotics in Germany. Carry a signed doctor's note.

Packing Medicines

German *Drogerien* (chemists) don't sell medication, not even aspirin. *Rezeptfrei* (over-the-counter) medications for minor health concerns only come from an *Apotheke* (pharmacy) and are likely more expensive than you expect. Pack enough pills for aches, pains and allergies, and birth control (prescription only).

Tap Water

Germany's *Leitungswasser* (tap water) is clean, drinkable and well filtered. Consider the source: alpine and mountain springs promise only regional excellence on tap. Surprisingly, Germans do tend to order bottled water in restaurants, but don't feel shy about asking for tap water. You may have to pay a small surcharge (€0.50 to €2) per glass, while a 0.5L bottle of water will cost €3 to €4.

TOILETS

Restaurants and bars don't have public toilets; you'll often have to pay. Malls, clubs and beer gardens often have attendants, who'll expect a tip (€0.20 to €0.50).

QUICK INFO

Herbertstrasse
This window prostitution street is restricted to adult males only (no women or minors).

Privacy
Only photograph people with permission. Some clubs forbid photography.

Marijuana
Cannabis possession is not illegal, but public consumption is.

Responsible Travel

Follow these tips to leave a lighter footprint, support local businesses and have a positive impact on communities.

Pfand System

In high-capacity venues, such as concerts, beer gardens, Christmas markets and nightclubs, you'll encounter Germany's *Pfand* (deposit) system, which aims to keep public spaces tidy and prevent waste. For drinks in reusable plastic glasses you'll pay a deposit (usually €1 per glass) and get a plastic token. Return the glass and, crucially, the token to the bar to get your deposit back, usually in change even if you've paid by card.

Get on Your Bike

Download the StadtRad Hamburg app and pick up a bike from red docking stations. The first 30 minutes of every ride are free, then it's €0.10 per minute or €24 per day.

OUR PICK ★

Be a Shoreline Hero

Join a community clean-up on Hamburg's rivers and canals. These volunteer events make for a nice afternoon with locals. Visit *cleanupyouralster.de* and *oclean.hamburg*.

How to Recycle

If you're staying in a residential building, be mindful of how Hamburg's eco-conscious locals recycle. Germany uses a colour-coded system: yellow (plastic, aluminium), blue (paper), brown (organic waste) and black/grey (non-recyclables) bins are set up next to the dumpster. Recycling correctly is serious; blatant disregard can attract a dressing-down from locals.

Resources

- *germany.travel/en/feel-good/sustainability* Official resource for low-carbon German travel.
- *umweltbundesamt.de/en* Federal environmental agency.
- *greensign.de* Certifies and lists sustainable hotels.

CLIMATE GOALS

Germany aims to become climate neutral by 2045 and to reduce greenhouse gas emissions by 65% by 2030. Hamburg aims for climate neutrality five years earlier. City-specific measures mean it's considered more likely to meet its target.

Sustainable Future

In recent years the Social Democratic Party (SPD) has relied on a coalition with the Greens to hold power in Hamburg, so the city has built a reputation for sustainable government. Mandated eco-development represents a societal choice. It's also a necessary one: climate change poses serious threats to a port city prone to extreme weather. Visit the **HafenCity InfoCenter** and the growing sustainable district **Wilhelmsburg** to see how green policy is shaping the landscape.

Climate Change & Travel

It's impossible to ignore the impact we have when travelling; Lonely Planet urges all travellers to engage with their travel carbon footprint, which will mainly come from air travel. While there often isn't an alternative, travellers can look to minimise the number of flights they take, opt for newer aircrafts and use cleaner ground transport, such as trains. One proposed solution – purchasing carbon offsets – unfortunately does not cancel out the impact of individual flights. While most destinations will depend on air travel for the foreseeable future, for now, pursuing ground-based travel where possible is the best course of action.

THE WEIGHT OF AMBITION

The UN Sustainable Development Report ranks Germany as fourth worldwide for its commitment to renewables, efficient public transport and emissions-busting innovation. The country has set ambitious climate goals; achieving them is a well-publicised, ongoing struggle.

The **UN Carbon Offset Calculator** shows how flying impacts a household's emissions

The **ICAO's carbon emissions calculator** allows visitors to analyse the CO2 generated by point-to-point journeys

Accessible Travel

Public Transport
Hamburg is fairly progressive when it comes to barrier-free travel. Access ramps and/or lifts are available, as is designated seating on board. Some stations have grooved platform borders to assist visually impaired passengers to navigate. Seeing-eye dogs are allowed on all public transport. Upcoming station names are typically displayed electronically on public transport.

Inclusive Sightseeing
Miniatur Wunderland (p88) offers evening hours during Wheelchair Mondays once or twice a month. The initiative aims to provide an accessible experience at an otherwise crowded museum. The **Internationales Maritimes Museum** (p87) provides tours tailored to those with visual impairments.

Restaurants & Museums
Access ramps and/or lifts are available in many public buildings, including museums, concert halls and cinemas. Many restaurants are also designed for accessibility, with ground-level entrances and wheelchair-friendly amenities.

ACCOMMODATION
Hamburg has a wide range of hotels with accessible features including lifts and rooms with extra-wide doors. Sustainable options include the barrier-free rooms at the **Reichshof**, which is fully green-energy powered.

OUR PICK

The **Dialoghaus** (Dialogue House, p96) exhibits Dialogue in Silence and Dialogue in the Dark allow visitors the opportunity to experience the daily life of people with visual and hearing impairments. On a one-hour tour, you'll be accompanied by a guide through dark or silent rooms to encounter everyday scenarios. The Hamburg-based social enterprise is active globally; the majority of staff have visible or invisible disabilities. Check the website for special events such as Dinner in the Dark.

--- **GETTING AROUND** ---

Some car-rental agencies offer hand-controlled vehicles and vans with wheelchair lifts at no charge (reserve well ahead). The **MOIA ride-pooling service** *(help.moia.io/hc/en-us)* offers vehicles with electro-hydraulic rear lifts and trained drivers.

Resources
- *hamburg-travel.com/barrier-free-travel* Hamburg Travel's website provides comprehensive lists of accessible lodgings and restaurants as well as city travel tips.

Nuts & Bolts

Opening Hours
The following are typical high-season opening hours in Hamburg.

Banks 9am to 4pm Monday to Friday, extended hours usually Tuesday and Thursday.

Major stores and supermarkets 9.30am to 8pm Monday to Saturday.

Boutiques and smaller stores 10am to 6pm Monday to Saturday.

Post offices 9am to 6pm Monday to Friday, to 1pm Saturday.

Museums Several are closed Monday.

QUICK INFO
Time zone
CET/UTC+1
Hamburg city code
040
Emergency numbers
fire & ambulance 112, police 110
Population
1.78 million

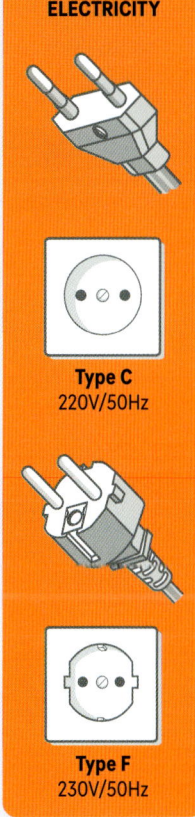

ELECTRICITY

Type C
220V/50Hz

Type F
230V/50Hz

Public Holidays
Germany observes four secular and eight religious public holidays, during which banks, shops, post offices and public services are closed. Unlike predominantly Catholic states such as Bavaria, Hamburg does not have additional regional holidays.

New Year's Day 1 January

Easter (Good Friday, Easter Sunday and Easter Monday) March/April

Ascension Day 40 days after Easter

Labour Day 1 May

Whit/Pentecost Sunday and Monday 50 days after Easter

Veterans Day 15 June

German Unity Day 3 October

Christmas Day 25 December

Second Day of Christmas 26 December

Smoking
Hamburg generally prohibits smoking in all indoor public spaces, but there's a key exception: *Raucherkneipen* (smoking pubs; small establishments under 75 sq metres that don't serve prepared meals and cater exclusively to adults). Some pubs have designated smoking rooms, but many allow patrons to light up freely.

Language

German Basics

Hello.
Guten Tag. *goo·ten tahk*

Goodbye.
Auf Wiedersehen. *owf vee·der·zay·en*

Yes.
Ja. *yah*

No.
Nein. *nain*

Please.
Bitte. *bi·te*

Thank you.
Danke. *dang·ke*

Excuse me.
Entschuldigung. *ent·shul·di·gung*

Sorry.
Entschuldigung. *ent·shul·di·gung*

Fast Phrases

Do you speak English?
Sprechen Sie Englisch? (pol) *shpre·khen zee eng·lish*
Sprichst du Englisch? (inf) *shprikhst doo eng·lish*
I don't understand.
Ich verstehe nicht. *ikh fer·shtay·e nikht*
Where's (the station)?
Wo ist (der Bahnhof). *vo ist (der bahn·hawf)*
What's the address?
Wie ist die Adresse? *vee ist dee a·dre·se*
Could you please write it down?
Könnten Sie das bitte aufschreiben? *kern·ten zee das bi·te owf·shrai·ben*
Can you show me (on the map)?
Können Sie es mir (auf der Karte) zeige *ker·nen zee es meer (owf dair kar·te) tsai·gen*
Help! Hilfe! *hil·fe*
Go away! Gehen Sie weg! *gay·en zee vek*
I'm ill. Ich bin krank. *ikh bin krangk*
Call the police! Rufen Sie die Polizei! *roo·fen zee dee po·li·tsai*
Call a doctor! Rufen Sie einen Arzt! *roo·fen zee ai·nen artst*
What time is it? Wie spät ist es? *vee shpayt ist es*
It's (10) o'clock. Es ist (zehn) Uhr. *es ist (tsayn) oor*
morning Morgen *mor·gen*
afternoon Nachmittag *nahkh·mi·tahk*
evening Abend *ah·bent*

Numbers

 eins *ains*

 zwei *tsvai*

 drei *drai*

 vier *feer*

 fünf *fünf*

 **Sound Like a Local**

Hey! Hey! *hei*
Great! Toll! *tol*
Cool! Spitze! *shpi·tse*
No problem. Kein Problem. *kain pro·blaym*
Sure. Klar! *klahr*
Maybe. Vielleicht. *fi·laikht*
No way! Auf keinen Fall! *owf kai·nen fal*
It's OK. Alles klar. *a·les klahr*
What a pity! Schade! *shah·de*
Doesn't matter. Macht Nichts. *makht nikhts*

> **DONATIONS TO ENGLISH**
>
> Numerous – you may recognise kindergarten, kitsch, waltz, hamburger, poodle.

 Signs

Ausgang Exit
Eingang Entrance
Damen Women
Herren Men
Heiß Hot
Kalt Cold
Offen Open
Geschlossen Closed
Kein Zutritt No Entry
Rauchen Verboten No Smoking
Verboten Prohibited

 **German in the World**

It's not usually described as romantic, but its role in science has long been recognised, and the German language lays claim to some of the most famous works ever printed – just think of the influence of Goethe, Nietzsche, Freud and Einstein.

--- **WHY BOTHER** ---

Don't be put off by the fact that German tends to join words together to express a single notion – it's not hard to tell parts of words, and you'll have fun recognising 'the Football World Cup qualifying match' hidden within *Fussballweltmeisterschaftsqualifikationsspiel*.

False Friends

Warning: many German words look like English words but have a different meaning altogether, eg *Chef* is boss, not *chef* (which is *Koch* in German).

 6 sechs *zeks*

 7 sieben *zee·ben*

 8 acht *akht*

 9 neun *noyn*

 10 zehn *tsayn*

Index

Sights p000   Map pages p000

See also separate subindexes for:
- 🍴 **Eating p158**
- 🍺 **Drinking p159**
- 🛍 **Shopping p159**

A
accessible travel 152
accommodation 25, 133, 145, 152
activities
   Discover Hamburg tour 51
   Hamburg Walks 51
   jungfernstieg promenade 66
   Kunstmeile 48
   Zweiradperle 50
allergies 146
Alsterarkaden 61
Alstertor 51
Altes Mädchen 138
Altonaer Balkon 136
Altonaer Museum 135
Altona 127-41, **128-9**
   drinking 140-1
   food 140
   shopping 141
   top experiences 130-3
   transport 127
   walking tour 134-5, **134**
Altstadt 35-53, **36-7**
   drinking 53
   food 52
   shopping 53
   top experiences 38-43
   transport 35
   walking tour 44-5, **44**
architecture 6-7, 46, 50
arriving 26
art galleries 10-11
Auswanderer-museum BallinStadt 58

B
Baakenpark 98, 99
Beatles-Platz 113, 116
Biergarten Speersort 49-50
biking, see cycling
Black Form 136
Brahms Museum 63
breweries 30, 147
Bucerius Kunst Forum 48
Bunny Burlesque 116

bus travel 28

C
Café Gnosa 79
cannabis 149
Cap San Diego 121
car rental 28, 152
car sharing 28
Cascadas 50
children, travel with, *see* family travel
Chilehaus 45
Chocoversum 49
Christmas Market 25, 118
climate change 95, 151
Clouds 118, 123, 124
costs 23, 29, 145, 147
Cotton Club 66
crime 22, 149
cycling 27, 150

D
Davidwache police station 113
Deichgraf 47
Deichstrasse 41, 45, 47, 90
Deichtorhallen 47, 48
Denkmal für Polnische Juden 135, 137
deposits 150
Deutsches Schauspielhaus Theatre 78
Deutsches Zollmuseum 99
Deutsches Zusatzstoffmuseum 98
Dialoghaus 96
disabilities, travellers with, *see* accessible travel
Dockland office complex 131
Docks Prinzenbar 117
drinking 8, 13, 30, 146-7, *see also individual neighbourhoods,* Drinking *subindex*

E
Elbjazz 24

Elbmeile 127-41, 128-9
   drinking 140-1
   food 140
   shopping 141
   top experiences 130-3
   transport 127
   walking tour 134-5, **134**
Elbmeile promenade 106, 130
Elbphilharmonie 89-91, 93, 97, 131
Elbphilharmonie Plaza 98
Elbstrand 130
electricity 153
emergency numbers 153
e-scooters 27

F
Fabrik 139
family travel 17, 144
FC St Pauli-Museum 113, 118-9
ferry travel 28, 133
festivals & events 24-5
   Christmas Market 25
   German Burlesque Festival 24
   Hamburger Dom 25, 111
   Port Anniversary 91
   Senatsbock 138
   St Pauli Food Truck Festival 25, 118
Fischerhaus 121
Fischmarkt 106-8, 130
Flohschanze 116
food 8, 30, 146-7, *see also individual neighbourhoods,* Eating *subindex*
Frau Hedi 121

G
Galerie Commeter 48, 51
gay travellers, *see* LGBTIQ+ travellers
Golden Cut 79
Gretel & Alfons 115, 124
Gröninger Privatbrauerei 45, 49
Grosse Freiheit 116

Grosse Freiheit party mile 113
Grossneumarkt 63, 65, 67
Gruenspan 117

H

Hafenbasar 93
HafenCity 85-101, **86**
  drinking 100-1
  food 100
  shopping 101
  top experiences 87-91
  transport 85
  walking tour 92-3, **92**
HafenCity InfoCenter 93, 95, 96
Hamburg Bunker 109-11, 113
Hamburg Card 23, 29
Hamburg Cruise Center 26
Hamburger Dom 25, 111
Hamburger Kunsthalle 43, 48
Hamburger SV City StorE 46
Hamburg's Staatsoper 66
Hansaplatz 77, 80
Harry's Hamburger Hafenbasar & Museum 95, 98
health 149
Heilige Dreieinigkeitskirche 77
highlights 6-17
  Altona & the Elbmeile 130-3
  Altstadt 38-43
  Neustadt 58-63
  Speicherstadt & HafenCity 87-91
  St Georg 74-5
  St Pauli & the Reeperbahn 106-11
history 31, 44-5
  Beatles 113, 115, 116-17, 121
  brewing 45
  commerce 99
  Jewish history 139
  maritime 87
  Protestantism 49
  WWII 42, 109-11, 135
Hobenköök 93, 96
Hoellanderischer Bluemenkonig 108
Holzbrücke 89
Hummel Memorial 65
Hummerstand im Hanseviertel 65

I

immigration 79

Indra Club 113, 125
Internationales Maritimes Museum 87, 93, 133
itineraries 18-21, 44-5, 64-5, 76-7, 92-3, 112-13, 114-15, 134-5

J

jazz 9, 24, 119-20
jungfernstieg promenade 61, 66

K

Kaffeemuseum Burg 97
Klippkroog 135
Kneipe 13, 118, 147
Knust 117
KomponistenQuartier 62-3, 65, 63-4
Kontorhaus District 46, 47
Koppel 66 77, 79
Krameramt-Witwen-Wohnung 66
Kunstmeile 48
Kunstverein 48

L

Laeiszhalle 67
Lange Reihe 77, 78
language 23, 146, 154-5
Laufauf 50
LGBTIQ+ travellers 82, 145, 148

M

Mahnmal St Nikolai 40-2, 41-3, 42-4, 45, 51
marijuana 149
Maritime Circle Line 133
markets 12
  Christmas Market 25, 118
  Grossneumarkt 67
  Hobenköök 93, 96
  St Pauli Nachtmarkt 113, 117
  Wochenmarkt 77
medications 149
Medizinhistorisches Museum 98
Miniatur Wunderland 88, 93
Mojo Club 119
Molotow 120
money 22, 23
Museum für Kunst und Gewerbe 48
museums 30-1

Museumshafen Oevelgönne 130
music, festivals 24
  Elbjazz 24
  Hamburger Kabarett-Festival 24, 119
  Reeperbahn Festival 24, 119
  Schlagermove 25, 119
music, live 9, 117
  Cotton Club 66
  Indra Club 113, 125
  Mojo Club 119
  Molotow 120
  St Michaelis Kirche 60
  Uebel & Gefaehrlich 111

N

Neustadt 55-69, **56-7**
  drinking 68-9
  food 68
  shopping 69
  top experiences 58-63
  transport 55
  walking tour 64-5, **64**
nightlife 9, 16, 30, 145, 146-7, 148

O

Oberhafen Kantine 96
Olivias Krawallschachtel 116
Olivias Wilde Jungs 116
opening hours 147, 153
Övelgönne 133

P

Park Fiction 122
parks & gardens 31
peak travel times 29
Pelikan Apotheke 65
Phoxxi Green Area 48
planning 22-3
Poggenmühlen Brücke 93, 94
population 153
Pride parade 148
privacy 149
prostitution 149
public holidays 153
public transport 27, 28, 144, 152

R

Rathaus 38-9, 45, 51
Ratsherrn brewery 138
recycling 150

Reeperbahn 103-25, **104-5**
   drinking 124-5
   food 123
   shopping 125
   top experiences 106-11
   transport 103
   walking tours 112-13, 114-15, **112, 114**
responsible travel 150-1
Restaurant Rustikal 121
rideshare 26
Rote Flora 136

S

safe travel 149
Senatsbock 138
shopping 12, 14-15, 148, *see also individual neighbourhoods*, Shopping *subindex*
smoking 153
Speicherstadt 85-101, 86
   drinking 100-1
   food 100
   shopping 101
   top experiences 87-91
   transport 85
   walking tour 92-3, **92**
Speicherstadtmuseum 93, 94
Spicy's Gewürzmuseum 97-8
Spielbudenplatz 113, 117-18
Star Club memorial 121
St Katharinen Kirche 46
St Georg 71-83, **72-3**
   drinking 82-3
   food 81-2
   shopping 83
   top experiences 74-5
   transport 71
   walking tour 76-7, **76**
St Marien-Dom 80
St Michaelis Kirche 58-60
St Pauli Nachtmarkt 113, 117
St Pauli Piers 130
St Pauli 103-25, **104-5**
   drinking 124-5
   food 123
   shopping 125
   top experiences 106-11
   transport 103
   walking tours 112-13, 114-15, **112, 114**
St Petri Kirche 48
StrandPauli 120
sustainability 151

T

Tanzende Türme 118, 123
taxi travel 26, 28
Thämer's 63, 65
time 23, 153
tipping 23
toilets 149
train travel 26, 28, 29, 144
tram travel 28
transport 26, 27-9
travel seasons 24-5

U

Uber 28
Uebel & Gefaehrlich 111

V

vegan travellers 146
vegetarian travellers 146
Viktoria-Kaserne 137

W

walking 27
water, drinking 149
weather 24
Wilhelmsburg 58
Wochenmarkt 77, 78

Z

Zeise Kino 138
Zur Ritze 115, 117
Zweiradperle 50

 Eating

A

Ahoi by Steffen Henssler 52
Alex 68
Atlantik Fisch 140

B

Bootshaus Grill & Bar 100
Brücke 10 123
Bullerei 140
Buttercrumbs Bakery 123

C

Cafe Gitane 81
Café Koppel 81
Café Mikkels 135
Café Mimosa 113, 123
Café Paris 39, 45, 52
Carls Brasserie 90, 100
Casa di Roma 81
Casse Croute 68
Chingu 52
Chopan 82
Cox 81

D

Daniel Wischer 52
Das Dorf 81

E

Eisliebe 140

F

Fleetschlösschen 100
Flying Market 140
Fräulein Fritz 81

G

Giovanni Rocco 115, 123

I

Injera 82

K

Kartoffelkeller 52
Kleine Haie Grosse Fische 115, 123
Kleine Pause 123
Konditorei Holger Rönnfeld 123

L

L'Amira 82
Lusitano 68

M

Matsumi 68
Minus 140
Mö-Grill 52
Mutterland Stammhaus 77, 81

N

Nardo's 52
Nil 123

O

Old Commercial Room 59, 68
Otto's Burger 81

P

Perle 52
Petit Bonheur 68

R
Ramen 52
Restaurant Herr He 82
Restaurant Rustikal 121
Rindermarkthalle 110, 123

S
Singh 82
Strauchs Falco 100

T
Table 100
Tide 140
Trific 52

Y
Yume Ramen 81

Z
Zum Spätzle 68

 Drinking

B
Bar Hamburg 82
Bar Kunterbunt 82
Bohemian 53

C
Cafe Geyer 107, 124
Café Knuth 140
Café Mikkels 140
Clockers 124
Clouds Bar 124
Constant Grind 124

F
Familien-Eck 135, 141
Frau Möller 83

G
Generation Bar 82
Golden Pudel Club 124

H
Herr Buhbe 68

I
Indra Club 113, 117

K
Kaffeeklappe at Speicherstadt-museum 101
Kaffeemuseum Burg 100
Kaiserkeller 117, 125
Katze 141
Komet 125
Kyti Voo 77, 83

L
Le Lion 53
Lunacy 125

M
M&V Bar 82

N
Nord Coast Coffee Roasters 53

O
Olivia Jones Bar 115, 116, 124
Olivias Kiez Oase 124

P
Palang Good Coffee 53
Pick Up 82
Public Coffee Roasters 69

R
Reh Bar 141

S
Speicherstadt Coffee Roastery 100
St Pauli Eck 115, 124

T
Tom's Saloon 82
Tower Bar 124

W
WunderBar 125

Z
Zum Schellfischposten 141
Zum Silbersack 115, 124

 Shopping

2nd Fit 141

A
Anne Zimmer 69
Apropos the Concept Store 69
Art of Hamburg 83
Atelier Figurart 83

B
B.Sweet 141
Blendwerk 83

C
Chapeau St Georg 83
Crazy Jeans 125

D
Dr Götze Land & Karte 51, 53

F
Flohschanze 125

G
Geigenbau Matthias Tödtmann 69
Geigenbau von Ketelhodt 65, 69
Geigenbau Winterling 69
Groove City 125

H
Hafen-Spezerei 101

K
Kaufhaus Hamburg 83
Kuestensilber Concept Store 101

L
Loonies 125

M
Mutterland 69

O
Otaku Records 125

S
Søstrene Grene 135, 141

T
Thalia 53
Tobias Strauch Weinkontor 69
Tutti Fagotti 69

V
Vintage & Rags 53
Vintage Revivals 141

W
Weinkauf St Georg 83
Wohnkultur 66 141

Z
Zardoz Records 125

Send Us Your Feedback

We love to hear from travellers – your comments help make our books better. We read every word, and we guarantee that your feedback goes straight to the authors. Visit lonelyplanet.com/contact to submit your updates and suggestions.

Note: We may edit, reproduce and incorporate your comments in Lonely Planet products such as guidebooks, websites and digital products, so let us know if you are happy to have your name acknowledged. For a copy of our privacy policy visit lonelyplanet.com/legal.

Acknowledgements

Cover photograph:
Speicherstadt (p85).
Olena Malik/Getty Images

Back photograph:
Hamburg Bunker (p109).
Taljat David/Shutterstock

THIS BOOK

The 3rd edition of Lonely Planet's Hamburg guidebook was researched and written by Barbara Woolsey. The previous edition was written by Anthony Ham. This guidebook was produced by the following:

Destination Editor
Sandie Kestell

Coordinating Editor
Sarah Bailey

Cartographer
Dorothy Davidson

Production Editor
Jennifer McCann

Image Editor
Clara Monitto

Assisting Editors
Clifton Wilkinson

Cover Researcher
Daisy Korpics

Thanks to
Ronan Abayawickrema, Alison Killea, Kellie Langdon, Darren O'Connell

Although the authors and Lonely Planet have taken all reasonable care in preparing this book, we make no warranty about the accuracy or completeness of its content and, to the maximum extent permitted, disclaim all liability arising from its use.

All rights reserved. No part of this publication may be copied, stored in a retrieval system, or transmitted in any form by any means, electronic, mechanical, recording or otherwise, except brief extracts for the purpose of review, and no part of this publication may be sold or hired, without the written permission of the publisher. Lonely Planet and the Lonely Planet logo are trademarks of Lonely Planet and are registered in the US Patent and Trademark Office and in other countries. Lonely Planet does not allow its name or logo to be appropriated by commercial establishments, such as retailers, restaurants or hotels. Please let us know of any misuses: lonelyplanet.com/legal/intellectual-property.

Paper in this book is certified against the Forest Stewardship Council™ standards. FSC™ promotes environmentally responsible, socially beneficial and economically viable management of the world's forests.

Published by Lonely Planet Global Limited
CRN 554153
3rd edition – Apr 2026
ISBN 978 1 83758 433 8
© Lonely Planet 2026
10 9 8 7 6 5 4 3 2 1
Printed in China